MRS. CHARLES

Hi. My name is Manali Jangid. You are absolutely allowed to call me 'MJ'.

I am a human just like you, but there's a twist. If you're seeking me, look no further than the pages between poetry and reality. Now that you are reading this book, I'm certain you've made a wise choice, setting it apart from the countless distractions of the moment. Your decision to choose me is a bequest to your astute taste and curiosity.

I am truly grateful for your efforts.

There are infinite stories that humans carry within their minds, and these stories become vividly apparent through the look in their beautiful eyes. I once read that *"the average person encounters around 80,000 to 1, 00,000 people in their lifetime."* This figure varies from person to person, but imagine if we could pause for a moment and delve into the stories that flow from each person's gaze. To comprehend even a fraction of these stories would take us several lifetimes, which in itself is nothing short of miracle. This thought has amazed me to the core and made me sit on the couch with a pen to write.

As I embarked on writing this book, my thoughts steered through countless energies and ideas, seeking answers to questions that often leave seekers at the edge of uncertainty and on the last stair of mystery. The deeper I pored over these reflections, the closer I came to understanding a new reality. The pages you are about to read reflect everything I imagined about a couple, known in my narrative as 'Charles', living in a parallel universe where the ordinary intertwines with the extraordinary.

My journey with this story began during my college years. The characters *'Matt and Jill'* initially captured my imagination, and from there, I embarked on transforming their lives into a work of art. Over time, the plot evolved to encompass the pre- and post-COVID-19 eras, mirroring the world's shifts and transformations. You may understand by now that I took quite a time to release to put my visualization in the form of a book.

It was through the encouragement of friends that I came to appreciate the importance of building an imagination and sailed this ship.

This book is a journey into the field of fiction, a canvas where fantasy paints the story of a family residing in 'New York City'. It explores their love for each other and uncovers the secrets that their home holds within its walls. As you read, you will find yourself immersed in the nuances of their lives, the trials they face, and the mysteries that surround them. The couple gave birth to triplets but after the loss on one, they were left with twins, *'Laxie and Macy'*, who bring depth and complexity to the story.

As I write these words, I am seated in my room, listening to the soothing patter of rain and holding a cup of cold coffee, which adds a sense of calm to my reflections. This setting mirrors the quiet contemplation that has shaped the story you are about to experience.

This book is dedicated to every reader in search of a compelling story that touches long after the last page is turned. I hope it captivates your attention and draws you into the world I've created. Get yourself a good pizza, and eat it while navigating the mystical and enthralling pages that lie ahead.

Warm regards

It was December 25, 2011 and *New York City* was full of 'life and lights'. New Year was around the corner and the street vibes were special in their own ways. People were rejoicing on the roads, savoring the fest, shopping things, clicking pictures, distributing holiday sweets, decorating the walls, dancing and singing altogether. The spirit of Christmas was evident everywhere and the neighborhood was famous for its over-the-top Christmas decorations, with houses adorned with countless lights and festive displays. Perfect life! That's what everyone thought including **Mrs. Charles**. Oh, you don't know her, of course. Let me introduce this lovely couple to you.

Meet Matt and Jill, ordinarily known as 'Mr. and Mrs. Charles'. They belonged to one of the happiest families of that time and were highly respected in their community because of the humbleness they carried within. Now, why am I mentioning 'happiest' here? Because life seemed complete for them. They were unique in their own ways and were blessed with a self-sufficient house, two beautiful girls, healthy lifestyle, work life balance and every possible luxury.

Talking about Jill, she was a charming woman who embodied warmth and friendliness in every interaction. Approached others with genuine compassion, she was always ready to lend a listening ear. Her empathy shined through as she understood and shared the feelings of those around her, provided comfort and support during both joyful and challenging times. She even created a nurturing and uplifting presence that enriched the lives of everyone she met. For her outer appearance, her wardrobe was full of corsets and long frocks, undoubtedly, women around had a lady crush on her.

Matt was a loving husband and super nice man. Honesty and truthfulness defined his communication. He approached life challenges with a constructive and respectful attitude. His positive outlook and cheerful presence not only brightened the lives of those he interacted with but also created a sense of trust and warmth wherever he went. On addition to this, he was a perfect father. Well, no one is perfect but Matt was and obviously that's not how anyone is supposed to be introduced but you know, this was his 'A' category quality.

Everyone saw Matt and Jill as a perfect couple and even idealized them. Some even said, *"If one of them dies, the other will die too, because they are meant for each other – even if it means they will be together in the afterlife."* They both gave birth to triplets but one of them passed away after living for two days. Fortunately, they were left with twin girls, later named as *Macy and Laxie*. Both of them had identical faces, similar placements of eyes, nose and mouth and their striking resemblance. Their deep bond fostered a unique sense of companionship where mutual support and understanding were central. Well, well, this was just the beginning.

Now coming back to the fest. Like all the people around, Charles' too were enjoying the street show in the heart of city. "Two candies please", Jill said. Vendor looked up and then shifted his head, tangentially. He wore his old fashioned spectacles to take a closer look of his customer. Jill was standing while holding the handle of the open umbrella in one hand, wearing an emerald green colored jacket, black pants and brown boots. Her left hand had a large-dial watch and index finger on her right hand had a heart shaped mauve wedding ring.

"Jill, Hey! Long time?" the old vendor said. Jill tilted her umbrella to see the face behind the voice. "Hey! Uncle. You recognized me?" she asked with an excitement. "How are you?" she questioned. "I am good..How come..you're here?" he asked with a hesitation in his voice. "Where is your husband and children?" he continued speaking while adjusting the jars kept in front of him and settling the awkwardness in the air. Jill smiled and replied, "We are here to enjoy the lights. And family is fine. They are reveling in the street show".

It was clear from their conversation that the vendor absolutely adored her family. He used to live in their locality four years ago but due to certain conditions, he sold his house and re-started his life with meagre earnings. Had no child of his own so he spent quarter of his life in the hope of having a child and next quarter in loving others'. He opened the jar and exchanged the candies with 2 dollars. "Have a great day, uncle and please visit us whenever you can", she said with a compassion in her voice. "Sure, Sure!" he replied and closed the jar lid.

She then presented those candies to her two beautiful

daughters who were watching the street performers playing their guitars. "Hey! Macy, Laxie! Look what I got for you", she said in a gentle voice. "Woah!" said Macy with her shining big eyes. "Thank you, Mommy", both of them replied with a smile on their faces. Macy and Laxie had beautiful blue eyes, taken after their father. Both of them loved wearing same dresses so whenever their mother used to go for a shopping, she generally bought the pairs. Same shoes, same socks, same hair bands, same skirts, same friendship bands. Everything, the same.

"Can I ask you a question?" Laxie said while facing Macy. "Nooooo", Macy responded while licking her candy. Laxie smirked and asserted, "I'm going to ask you anyways and you have to answer it, earlier was just my polite gesture towards you". Macy kept her focus on the candy. "Okay, who do you think Mom and Dad love the most?" Laxie questioned despite her sister's constant ignorance. "As in?" Macy asked with a confusion in her voice and eyebrows dramatically raised.

Before Laxie could think of explaining, their mother sat down on her knees and said "Mommy too wants to eat the candy." Macy jumped and said, "You can share it with me". Laxie could not bear the second place, so she ordered furiously "No mom, take mine".

Hearing their constant leg pulling, Jill grinned and stood up saying, "I was just joking. I know you guys earned this candy by studying super hard in pre finals. Let's go back home. We will eat our dinner and celebrate the eve, together", she said while

Macy and Laxie were seen smiling at each other. Meanwhile, Jill started searching for her husband. Seeing him, she called out his name loudly, "Matt. Matt, come let's go." Matt immediately looked at her and his lips moved "One second" with his index finger raised in the air. Jill and girls stood near the lamppost and Matt walked to her, "Glittery balloons for my shining wife". Seeing which, she started blushing and held the string of white thread tightly in her hand.

See, I told you right? This was a happy family. The family of everyone's dreams including the vendor who ran a few errands to earn a living but couldn't bore a child and always felt the void in his life. Laxie and Macy were not just sisters but also each other's best friends. Well, what are twins for? They took birth, opened their eyes for the first time, started walking, speaking, everything altogether.

After waiting for five minutes, all of them sat in the car and headed towards their home. "What is the timing of your meeting, tomorrow?" Jill asked while adjusting her seat belt. "7:00 AM", Matt answered. "Oh, that means I am supposed to wake up around 5. I feel so lazy already", she replied while leaning her head on the headrest. "It's absolutely okay, I'll grab a bun from the canteen & you, my love, can rest properly. From past few days, you have been running on your toes", he assured. "Nope, I was joking. I'll prepare everything before you leave" she replied like any man would dream of. "I know you're Mrs. Perfect for all the right reasons", he answered while looking at her. "Hey, but what about Jimmy? Why is she not coming these days? Actually this came in my mind earlier but I forgot to ask you or probably I did, I don't remember clearly", he kept speaking while his one eye was on the road and other was on his wife. "She isn't well and I talked to her son this morning itself, it will take some time for her to recover and till then, I'm your new cook, Sir", she spoke with a smile on her face and index finger pointing towards her greek nose. The car was moving at a safe speed while they were discussing the entire scenario. "What happened to her?" he questioned while changing the gear. "Her son informed that she fell from stairs and is now receiving treatment to recover", she replied while removing the seat belt. "Oh! Tell him to consider us if they need any kind of help" he replied while applying the car brakes in front of their house.

The house was fifth from the left on 'DY Street', next to Darry's house. Darry was one of the wealthiest men in the locality. And why was he famous? Because he had his own talk show and publishers were crazy behind his podcast stories. His book even got nominated twice in an award show and cameras were always seen running after him. Matt personally liked him for his hard work and all that he earned at such a young age.

"Home sweet home", said Jill while looking at the main door. Charles' named their home as 'Fragrance' which got its name after Matt's mother. When he was too young to even go out and earn a living, he decided his house's name which later turned into a 'Home' because each corner inside, brought warmth and peace. Explaining its structure, it was a 2 floored mansion painted off-white. Earlier it was salmon pink but the woman of the home gave a touch to it by choosing the color of her own. She thought her life was like a canvas and whatever color was poured on it, created a beautiful painting.

There were four windows on the front wall, each present at a distant space and were of a moderate length. The door had this nameplate displaying "*Mrs. & Mr. Charles*." They were actually breaking the monotonous cycle of 'Mr. Coming first before Mrs.'

"Let me park the car", he mentioned politely. Three of them came out and shut the doors synchronously. Macy and Laxie were still fighting on the same question. "No, they love me the most", Macy shouted. "You are lying, they are mine", Laxie answered with an absolute anger in her voice.

Macy and Laxie shared everything in common but they differ on only one thing. Macy was quiet and a settler. Laxie was bold and confidence reflected in her eyes. So, when it came to winning things, Laxie was a champion and if hearts, than Macy was already carrying it on her sleeves. "Why do you always think of winning, Laxie?" questioned Macy. "I don't know why you aren't accepting the visible facts", Laxie replied while moving her index finger under her nose. Hearing the chit chatter, their mother interrupted in between. She was holding the shopping bags in her right hand while her left hand was busy in searching for the keys in the purse. "Girls, what happened? Tell me", she questioned.

Laxie faced her mother and complained "Mom, tell Macy that you and daddy love me more than her." In the reaction, Macy threw her hands in the air and said "Mom". Jill looked at each one of them and replied, "We both love each one of you, equally and the depth is immeasurable. You are equivalent in our eyes and I'm definitely not liking this idea of indulging in a petty fight like this". "But mom, I am never interested in initiating such conversations. It was Laxie who started. In fact I even ignored her question but she is so persistent you know", said Macy while giving a stern expression.

Laxie started making faces after hearing all of that. "Mom, I'm at no fault. I was just asking a simple question which I believe was not wrong", she replied. "I believe both of you got the clear and steer answer. Now, don't fight and let me search our door keys", Jill said. Her expressions clearly reflected her concentration. 'Found!' Jill clicked the tongue and smiled. "Come, let's open the door", she said while walking towards the doorstep. While putting the key in the keyhole, she moved it in the clockwise direction and the lock opened, making all three to step inside.

"Go, get your dresses changed and come back fast. I want you both here within 10 minutes. Don't forget to wear the socks and place the hanger from where you take it. Okay?" Jill instructed and placed her purse on the table. Both the girls nodded their heads, ran towards their rooms jumping and giggling.

After few minutes, Matt opened the door and came straight to the kitchen. He held his wife in his arms and leaned his head to touch hers. She looked at him and asked "What?" to which he replied, "Thanks for bringing so many blessings in my life." She smiled and gave a warm hug by tightly wrapping her arms around him. Giving a peck on his lips, she mentioned "You are the best man I could ever ask from the universe." She then slightly pushed him and said "Did you lock the door?" to which he replied "Absolutely!" Jill looked at him and said "Now, go. I have to make our dinner and sleep on time. It's 11 already." He held the edge of kitchen slab and asked "Can I help you?" to which she replied while pointing diagonally, "Nope! I will be handling everything and your bathroom is that way, Sir". Matt winked at her and went inside the bedroom. He returned back questioning about the bill while holding an envelope in his hands "Darling, did you check this? The due date was 18th December and today is 25th" to which Jill replied "Yep, submitted". "Ok, I'll keep it in the Bills Box", he answered while checking the amount. "Don't leave the geyser on", she warned. "I am going to take a cold shower", he replied while placing the bill on the table. "You what?" she asked from a distance. "Kidding. I will do as you say", he replied while going back to their room and she jerked her head while cleaning the slab.

"Mommy", a voice came from upstairs. "Coming", Jill replied. She stood near the end of stairs and questioned, "What happened, Sweety?" Laxie was draped in a towel and while biting her lips, she inquired, "Mom, where is my nightdress?" to which Jill answered "It is in the right block of your cupboard".

"Can you come and find that for me?" Laxie requested while standing at a wider tread. "Baby, my hands are all occupied in work. Please find it and call me if there's any issue again", Jill replied and came back to the kitchen. Laxie took a deep breath and entered in her room. Few seconds passed and Jill's heart started to melt, knowing her daughter wasn't able to find something and needed her mother's help. She immediately washed her hands and went to Laxie's room. Laxie was still searching for the dress.

While looking at her, Jill started to think about the last place her night dress was kept. "I think I left it in Macy's room by mistake. Let me bring it for you" said Jill. "Wrap yourself", she continued speaking.

"Macy? Please open the door. I need something" said Jill while knocking the door. Hearing her mother's voice, Macy opened the door and Jill entered the room, headed straight towards the cupboard. "Macy, did you see your sister's night wear?" Jill questioned. "Nope! I haven't seen mine even" replied Macy while lying on her bed and playing with her doll. "Macy, why haven't you taken a shower yet?" Jill asked. "Because I feel sleepy, Mommy. Can I take a nap for a while? I'll have my dinner around 12" Macy requested.

"No, baby. You need to get into the bathroom right now and take your bath robe along. No wet floors, okay? And keep your doll near the bedside table" Jill ordered while pointing her finger towards the bathroom door. "Here, it is!" Jill smiled and left Macy's room. "Take this sweetheart and come downstairs, fast" Jill said while handing over the onesies to Laxie. It had been 10 years since the birth of the twins, and to the couple, these girls still seemed as small and precious as ever. Jill knocked at Macy's door after fifteen minutes and said "Macy, baby dinner is ready."

"I haven't changed my clothes, yet", said Jill to herself and went downstairs. While she was preparing the table, everyone gathered, Macy came with her favorite doll and sat on her chair. The family had an oval shaped dining table which added the look to their hall. "Grab a seat, you too", Matt told Jill while shifting his glass of water on the right side. It turned 12:30 AM till they finished their dinner. "No, I decorated the tree", Macy said while Laxie was teasing her uninterruptedly. "Give me your doll, it seems as if she needs a makeover" said Laxie. "No, I like her the way she is", replied Macy while hugging it tightly. "From now onwards, I will call you 'Tisty'", said Macy while looking at her doll. "I've got to go", Matt said firmly and stood up, placed his chair back to its place and went near the basin to wash his hands. Later wiped them using a hand towel and went back to his room. "Darling, I'll be working for some time. You can come as you finish the chores" to which Jill replied "Okay!" while taking a spoon of rice from her bowl. She took the plates to the kitchen sink and instructed the girls to go back to their beds. "School tomorrow", she said in an audible tone. At a later time, the lights were turned off and like her routine, she checked all the gates and went to her room.

Next morning, Jill woke up at 5:40 AM and prepared the breakfast for all three. She went to wake Matt up and said, "Matty, its 6:03, wake up now". After constant push, he woke up, left his bed and sat on the couch with a weary face. "Matt, wake up, you will be late", Jill repeatedly tried to make him stand on his feet. After regress efforts, he went to the bathroom and she went to Macy's room. "Get up twinkey", she asserted. "Mommy, 2 minutes more. I slept late", Macy replied. "No, you'll be late for school and teacher will scold you. Do you want the scolding?" questioned Jill. "No" replied Macy while hugging her tightly. "Come 'on now, I'm going to Laxie's room", Jill said and went inside the other daughter's room.

After entering Laxie's room, Jill was shocked to see her. "You're giving me surprises everyday" said Jill with a proud face. Laxie was standing in her uniform, tying a ribbon in her hair. "I am awake since the whole night", Laxie answered. "Why? Was anything troubling you?" Jill questioned. "No, I had some weird dreams. Something was not right around me", said Laxie. "I don't get you. What happened? Tell me", Jill asked with a panic visible in her expressions. "I had a dream where I lost my life to god and entered into the parallel world. Nothing was right there, everyone seemed crawling. All the faces were strange and their eyes were bulgy. I woke up and switched the lights on to feel the reality" Laxie explained. Knowing it was a dream, Jill smiled "It was just a bad feeling. Nothing else!" But Laxie looked at her and replied "It seemed real, Mommy". Jill hugged her and replied, "Dreams are just dreams until proved in real. You can sleep with your sister or us today. Okay?" Laxie smiled and hugged her back.

Jill walked downstairs while untying her apron. She hung it on the hook. Matt on the other hand, took his shirt out of the cupboard and closed it back. He then opened it again to look for a matching tie. "Jill, I cannot find my black tie. Please look it for me" he requested. "Coming!" Jill replied. He got ready, had his breakfast and left hastily. Obviously he woke up so late and ended up running towards the car. Jill waved her hands and said "Bye, babe!" Matt half smiled addressing the miles he had to cover in such short period of time. Told you, he was late!

Jill got ready for her own work and took both of her daughters to drop at their school. "This time we will be going for a picnic and it's a surprise. And that too on your birthday" said Jill with an excitement in her tone. "I want to know the place, Mommy. I'll dress up accordingly" said Laxie. "No, it's a secret and secrets are revealed when it is time. So, no hush push" replied Jill. Laxie whispered something in Macy's left ear and both of them started laughing. "What is it?" Jill questioned with curiosity. "It's a secret, Mommy", replied Laxie in a happy tone. Jill smiled and dropped them at main gate of the school. "Do not fight! I need no complaints" Jill demanded. Laxie and Macy ran towards the porch of the school and waved back at her. This was Jill's life. She loved doing things for her family and played the role of motherhood exceptionally well.

"Mommy, pick us at sharp 4" Laxie announced from a distance. "Why?" asked Jill with a serious expression and her index finger pointing upwards. "Because we will be having a mini party in our group, near the canteen", said Laxie. "Come here!" Jill ordered. Both of them came near their mother, "Who gave you the permission to party without any discussion?" added

Jill. "Macy, we discussed this right? With Mom" said Laxie. "Yeah", Macy replied in an obvious tone. "Mommy, we informed you yesterday in the car itself!" replied Laxie but now in a bossy way. Jill's face expressions turned into a confusion theory. She tried to recall but couldn't, "I don't remember, But..Okay', Jill replied. "Not beyond 4. I'll pick you from here. Now, get inside else you will be late", she suggested.

"What is happening to her? I informed her and you were there" said Laxie. "I don't know!" Macy whispered. Jill was watching both of them talking to each other about her. "Let's go", they said in unison. The girls were seen running away and Jill started questioning her senses "What is happening to me? I remember everything that we did yesterday but they didn't mention anything then how come..now..". This was the first time Jill was feeling this way. Never forgetting anything was her 'A-quality'. Okay, you now you must know but she was an all-rounder. She handled everything smoothly and was very much known for her photographic memory. "I can't believe myself. I think I should see Daisy before I leave for brunch at office" she suggested herself. Jill opened her car gate and sat inside. For the record, Jill and Matt had their own cars and that was an ultimate luxury. They handled everything equally, and Matt was clear about his definite support for prioritizing his wife's needs. After starting the car, she picked her phone and dialed Daisy's number.

Daisy is Jill's best friend since college and Matt was Daisy's friend from school. They both got admission in the same college and two days later, Jill joined the class. All three of them studied management course and pursued different courses for masters. Matt fancied Jill from the start and somehow it was Daisy's major role in their relationship. Love birds got serious and opened about each other to Jill's family and later on got married. Daisy was present from both the sides in the marriage but she chose to be the bridesmaid over anything else.

"Daisyyyy, pick up the phone" said Jill. She redialed her number and later, phone was finally answered. "Hello?" said Daisy. "Where are you?" Jill enquired. "Home" Daisy replied. "I am coming!" said Jill. She disconnected the call and put the phone on passenger seat. After applying the gears, she headed towards her best friend's home. Daisy lived half hour away from the girls' school.

After driving for twenty five minutes, she sensed someone else's presence in the car. She looked in the mirror and found nothing. Her eyes kept juggling between the mirror and the road. After slight assurance, she focused back on driving. "Maybe, I am overthinking. I need to take my sleep schedule seriously now." She nodded her head in agreement and took a left to park the car in Daisy's parking lot. She again looked in the mirror to confirm how she felt. "Overthinking kills!" Jill said in a sympathetic tone. She grabbed her purse and trench coat, opened and shut the car door, pressed lock button in her keys and started walking towards the main door. All the thoughts were moving in her head like a hurricane.

"Take a deep breath, tell everything to Daisy, and fix things and move on. Voila!" she reminded herself and pressed the door bell, twice, thrice, and there she was! "Hiyayayayayyayayay", said Daisy with an excitement. "Feels so great to see you" she added while hugging her. "I know! I missed you so much" Jill replied with a biggest smile on her face. It was 9:30 in the morning and sun was nowhere to be seen. Cold days, you see. December 26th. "By the way, Merry Christmas!" Daisy greeted. Jill gave a smile and replied, "Merry-Merry Christmas to you too!"

"You look beautiful in this fabric" Daisy commented fondly. "Thank you!" Jill replied while entering the house. "You changed your cushion covers" Jill said astonishingly. "Finally, it was time to let them go. Actually, Ginger scratched everything and the condition of the covers was so ugly, I felt mortified in the end", Daisy replied in a laughing tone. *Ginger* was Daisy's cat so short story, she was a cat mom and had no plans to get married or settle down. Daisy had a habit of holding on the things for longer than usual and that was the reason why she chose to keep the cushion covers even when they were tainted.

"Okay, what will you have? I was preparing my breakfast and I have omelette on bread, toast and sugar free orange juice to offer" Daisy boasted. "I have my brunch arranged at office", Jill replied while tightening her lips. "Oh come on woman! We are having our starters here" said Daisy.

Not to mention but Daisy was a great cook, her café made numbers and money eventually. "I'll have omelette, Ma'am and one second, what is this sugar free juice?" Jill asked with her eyebrows almost touching the hairline. "Nothing! I don't put sugar in the juice" replied Daisy laughingly. Jill smiled and both of them moved to her dining table.

Daisy had a charming house with a welcoming entrance featuring two large windows and a door in between. Her father, a skilled carpenter in his time, had crafted that door himself. Despite having three or four visible cracks, Daisy cherished it deeply as a sentimental reminder of her father's craftsmanship and their shared memories. Every time she passed through the door, she felt a sense of connection to her father's legacy and the warmth of her childhood home. Moving inside, left side of the wall was filled with her paintings and right side wall had pictures of her with the family including Jill. On the right, there were stairs leading to the roof. Straight ahead was a hall with a chandelier hanging from the ceiling. It was a dreamy one, believe me. She got that from Paris when she visited there for a cooking show. There were two rooms, one master bedroom and a kitchen, all of them spread in four different directions. The dining table was placed near the kitchen counter, allowing the cook to serve food directly from the stove. Jokes. Behind the dining area was a balcony that opened onto a garden where vegetables were grown by her.

"Is that a pumpkin?" Jill questioned while pointing towards the spot in the garden. "Yep, Maxima!" Daisy replied. "This is super nice and the shape seems perfect! You're acing it, girl", Jill said with an excitement hearing which, Daisy smiled.

"Well, I need to talk to you about something" said Jill while arranging the wine glasses on the table. "Hm, go ahead", Daisy replied while tasting the sauce from her spatula. "I'm having dreams", replied Jill. "Dreams?" Daisy questioned. Now, Jill was confused to move forward or not and was feeling slightly delusional for a moment. "Shall I say it?" said Jill. "Yeah", Daisy replied. "I feel someone is following me everywhere I go" said Jill in a terrifying voice. "Who?" Daisy asked while keeping the plate on the slab. "There's no physical entity. It's in the air", Jill replied. This statement made Daisy laugh her heart out. "Are you kidding me? Something in the air" said Daisy. "This story is stale to be sold and I'm definitely not buying it. Pff..you're seeing..and", Daisy started laughing again. Jill was taken aback by this reaction and felt a pang of heartbreak. She was not ready for this reaction as she travelled all the way to explain the scenario in person. Judging the atmosphere, she decided to keep her feelings to herself and changed the subject while trying to mask her emotions. "Daisy, why don't you find a partner for yourself? You're good looking, life seems fine and overall, you're earning well. Independency on the peak!" said Jill. Daisy rolled her eyes and spoke "I'm not made for any one. Maybe *Sologamy* is it, for me. You know", replied Daisy in a sarcastic tone. "Shut up!" replied Jill in a funny way.

"Now go and make an omelette for me. I need to leave for office and drive miles from here", she added. "Well, Ma'am your office isn't in San Jose. You'll drive fine" replied Daisy while turning the omelette on the pan. "Speaking of which, mom is moving in with me. It's her age and I personally want her to live with me and Ginger", said Daisy. "Okay, this is appreciated. Matt talks about her a lot. He misses her roasted turkey and I tried very hard to add some aroma but failed proudly. It's something in her hands, he says" replied Jill while remembering the days with Daisy's mother. "True that!" Daisy remarked.

After an hour of fun and laugh, Jill picked her bag and grabbed the water bottle to leave for the office. "I'm feeling so tired already", said Jill. "Well, well, this is new to me. Mrs. Charles never gets tired and today..strange!" Daisy replied. Jill knew if she said something now, it will cost her next 24 hours and now she somehow got over that bad dream cycle. "Yeah, human tendencies" replied Jill while unlocking the car. "Take care! And call me whenever you can. Do make sure you invite us when mom enters the city" said Jill. Daisy nodded her head in agreement and smiled peacefully.

While reversing the car, Jill was in a happy mood. Her day had a good start and she met her friend after a very long time. "Matt will be really happy, let me send him our picture", she slowed her car and tried to reach to her phone. "Where did I keep it? I think I forgot my phone. I think.." while she was talking to herself she again felt the same energy inside her car. She looked in the mirror to check if someone was sitting on the back seat but like it was evident, no one was there. Taking out her phone, she sent their picture to her husband and wrote "We missed you!" After keeping her phone on the passenger seat, she drove to her office. However, since she had the option to work remotely as a writer, she found it more convenient to stay home. She could sit on the veranda, enjoy a coffee, and work on her laptop at her leisure.

On days when there were pre-planned book releases or publishing dates, she visited the office which was on the '10th floor of NWY'. She parked her car, greeted the watchman and rushed towards the lift while checking time. The lift door finally opened and because of heavy rush, she was not able to find the space to stand. This building had multiple company offices on different floors. "What a mess?" she murmured. With much effort, she stepped out, cleaned her skirt and trench coat by moving her hands on it.

"Hello, Mrs. Charles", Bob greeted as she opened the door. "Good morning", Jill replied humbly. Bob was her cubicle partner and nearly forty eight years old. She went to her desk and suddenly her phone started to ring, "Come to my cabin, please", Boss mentioned. She panicked and reported inside his office. Actually, here "please" in his tone meant that "It is urgent and you have done a blunder".

"What's going on? Why isn't this report finished, and your article is still incomplete? Today was the deadline," he began to interrogate. Jill calmly replied, "Just two more hours, sir, and I'll have it done." She glanced at her boss's face, noticing his growing frustration.

Jill gave a smile and came outside while holding her id card. She went back to her desk and pulled out some piece of papers from the file and switched on her computer to complete her pending work. Jill was a hard working independent woman and worked in the *'Scthandley Co. & ltd.'* as a content writer for the articles and magazines. Her novels used to get published in New York, that time.

"Coffee?" asked Bob. "Of course! Make it strong, please. I need it" replied Jill. "Sure, Ma'am", Bob answered. He came after ten minutes, kept the paper cup near Jill's hand and started talking. "So, how was your Christmas this time? I heard the Christmas tree in 'Times Square' was so massive that people had to look up to see the top" said Bob. "I believe. It is one of my favorites. Well, I went nearby and we had fun too" replied Jill with a gentle smile and eyes glued on her computer. "How's Matt?" asked Bob. "He's amazing. Thank you so much for asking' replied Jill. "Like always!" Bob reacted with a tilted head and a cool look.

After some time, she stood up with a file in her hand and went to *'Jacob, The Boss'* and handed it to him saying, "It is completed, Sir. You can check on the final conclusions." Jacob didn't even bother to look up from his laptop. While working, he casually ordered the report to be published. Jill was stunned that he hadn't even proofread it before giving the go-ahead. So, she turned around and handed the file to Bob and told him to pass it to Mr. Cole for publishing. She again went back to her seat, and started checking her phone. A message popped up, it was from Matt enquiring about her day. She typed "Good but extremely busy", she kept the phone aside and started collecting the clips for her next article. "Why don't I write on self—Love? It will be the greatest idea possible. People are ending their lives because of loneliness and this article can be a thoughtful way to put an idea of love into words" Jill murmured.

It was 03:30 P.M. when she left for home. As she unlocked the car, she smelled a strange odor, almost like something was burning. "What is this smell?" she questioned and bent down to take a closer look of the surface under the car. "Never mind", she said to herself and sat on her seat. She was continuously thinking about the article and silently collecting the thoughts in her mind. "Work is worship," she affirmed to herself, clearing her mind of distractions.

She stopped the car to register a strong plot that came on her mind. 'We believe the world is changing day by day..' she started to type in her phone. While her thoughts were visible on the screen, she realized about the girls getting free at four. She immediately shifted the gears and turned the car towards the school's lane. There was the same strong energy in the car. She convinced herself that her imagination was playing tricks on her and there wasn't actually anything there. With this thought in mind, she arrived at the school to pick up her daughters.

To her surprise, the school gate was locked and both of them were standing outside. She came out of the car, took their bags in each hand and asked, "Why isn't anyone here? Where are all the children?" to which Laxie replied "They are all gone with their parents. It's past four, Mommy. School gate is closed now." Hearing all of this, Jill kept the bags in her car trunk, opened the gate for two girls to sit. "Mommy, I have got lots and lots of homework today", Laxie mentioned while she was opening her tie knot. Macy while drinking the water, corrected her, "We have got that."

"How come none of your friends waited", Jill questioned. "All of them left because it was getting late", Macy replied. "But its just 04:12 PM", Jill replied. "Just?" Laxie questioned. "Ok, so who wants to grab burgers, today?" asked Jill to divert the topic. "Meeeeee", replied Macy and Laxie. "I'll take the cheese one and I will tell this on the counter to add patty and lettuce in a good amount" said Laxie. "Okay!" replied Jill while rotating the car steering. She stopped the car near *'Clarke's'* and entered after ringing a bell which was hanging outside the door. Both the girls explained the customized orders to their mother and she went to pay the bill, collected the receipt and kept it in the purse. "So, how was your pa-aart-yy?" asked Jill in a comic tone. "It was great. You know Mommy, Sam wanted to snatch our ice creams and Laxie pushed him because I don't know who does that?" said Macy confusingly. "Our party was good, Mommy. We enjoyed a lot" said Laxie while trying to cover the incident. Jill enquired "Who is Sam? The one we met in your parent-teacher meeting last year?" to which Macy answered "Yes, he has an elder brother too. He is a bully. He snatches things from people and claims of owning them". "But you know, Mommy we are great together and we absolutely don't care what people do. We are honest, that's what we know" said Laxie. Jill was pleasantly surprised to see how maturely the 10-year-olds were talking. Both of them completed their "Happy Meals" and stepped out of the shop.

Jill drove back home and both the girls started playing *'Pen, paper and scissors'*, a popular game among children at that time. They made fun of each other on losing. "You lost it" said Laxie. "No, you are a liar" said Macy. With all the noise in the car, Jill's phone chimed. She unlocked her phone to find a message from her husband, Matt. It said, "I have an urgent trip out of town and will be home very late. Please take care of yourself and keep the doors locked. I'll keep you informed and share the location as well". This was common. Like Jill's brain gave lot of quality work, Matt's boss was totally reliable on him. From meetings to tours, Matt was always chosen on priority. "Okay, Love you!" Jill typed and pressed the accelerator pedal. After driving for few minutes, they reached their home.

Jill unlocked the door of her house and went inside. The girls followed her, jumping and hopping. She locked the door from inside and hanged the keys on the hook on the wall. "Complete your homework and show it to me before you start playing again. Hang your uniforms properly behind the door and wash yourself up" ordered Jill. "Okay, Mommy!" said Laxie and both the girls went upstairs. "I should take a nap" she said to herself. She went inside the bathroom, washed her face and hands, changed her dress and wore a comfortable one. While closing the curtains of her room, she laid on her bed.

Thoughts were unstoppable and out of all the chaos, she started to over think about everything. Her eyes were closed but the mind was boggled. "Shall I call Matt and tell him?" said Jill in a soft voice. "No, he must be busy" she added while turning her back towards the curtains. While looking at the almirah door, she closed her eyes. After sleeping for two whole hours, she woke up in a sundowned mood. "Still..oh god. Am I supposed to feel this way?" she said to herself. The burden of thoughts occupied her mind when she was supposed to be taking care of the house and managing her work. "Let it be", she said to herself and started checking her phone. Three missed calls from Matt, one from Ayra who was her neighbor and one from Jimmy's son. When she saw Ayra's name, she remembered her promise to go to the supermarket with her.

"Oh, no!" Jill said while calling Matt. "Let me talk to him, first" she said. His phone rang and after four rings, he picked up. "Hey!" said Matt. "Hey!" replied Jill in a low voice. "Where were you?" questioned Matt with a concern in his voice. "I was sleeping" replied Jill. "Wait, are you okay?" asked Matt. "Yeah, felt dizzy earlier so.." while she was completing her sentence Matt questioned, "Did you eat your lunch?" "Um, no" she replied with a heavy heart. "Babe, what happened? Why didn't you eat anything?" Matt asked. "I didn't feel like doing anything but yeah, I'm going to eat something now. I feel hungry" said Jill. "Yes and inform me once you eat something" said Matt. "By the way, I'm near my meeting hall and will call you in sometime. Don't miss the food. Okay? Love you! Bye!" he continued speaking. Matt ended the call, and Jill tried to reach Ayra by phone, but she didn't answer. Later, she called Jimmy's son and his phone was switched off. She stepped out of her bed, wore her slippers and went in the hall. "Macy, Laxie, where are you children?" Jill asked while crossing the hall.

There was silence and none of the girls answered. She again called their names but there wasn't any response. She tied her robe and climbed the stairs in panic. "Macy! Where are you? Laxie" she said in a loud tone while looking at her left and right. "Macy", saying this, she opened her room's door. No one was there. Jill's eyes got welled up. "Laxie", she entered in her room while her throat started choking. "Macy, Laxie" she repeated. "Yes, Mommy" came the reply.

Both the girls were sitting in their doll house and zip closed. Jill ran towards them and opened the zip. "What are you doing inside?" she asked while hugging both the girls. "Why were you not answering me?" she questioned while tears started to flow out of her eyes. "We didn't hear you in the first place" replied Laxie. Macy wiped the tears and said "Mommy, why are you crying?" Jill closed her eyes tightly and said "No, I am not but I was worried" said Jill. "But..you said we could play after we complete our homework so we did. See, our homework is on the study table. You can check" replied Laxie while pointing in the left direction. "I know. But.." said Jill. "Anyways, are you hungry?" Jill questioned. "No, Mommy. I'm full" replied Macy. "I can eat anything you make" replied Laxie. "I'm making oats" said Jill while looking at both of them. "No, Mommy. I'll eat nothing now. I'll take pomegranate juice" said Laxie. "Okay!" replied Jill as she stood up. She took an exit from Laxie's room and came again to check if they were safe. Laxie and Macy started playing again.

"What's wrong with me? They were simply playing in their rooms..infact I only told them to do so, then why", Jill was thinking while descending from the stairs. She entered into her kitchen, came back near the railing of the stairs and started staring at Laxie's room. "I can't be like this. I need to stop this..this..over thinking. Understand the gravity of the circumstances instead of making everything on my own. I am smart, I can handle things well, Laxie and Macy are happy" Jill started murmuring.

She turned around and went into her room. After opening her almirah, she pulled the left side drawer and took out the photo frame. It had her family's picture where Laxie was sitting on Matt's thigh and Macy was standing in front of Jill. The couple was sitting on a bench in a park nearby and it was drizzling that day. Laxie had a chocolate in her left hand and right hand was touching Matt's elbow. Macy was holding her favorite doll in both the hands and Jill's arms were around her neck. All of them were smiling. She hung the frame on the wall of the hallway, near the dining table, so everyone could see it all the time. "My love", said Jill.

Jill, like I mentioned before, was a family oriented person and believed in providing every good thing to her family. She could do anything to protect them and sometimes even did. Jill's parents never wanted her to marry Matt. His mother passed away when he was four and his father married someone else leaving him all alone. In his early years, he lived with his maternal uncle but later his family started having problems which forced Matt to move out of their place. When Jill met him, she knew it was 'Love at first sight' and after knowing about his past, she became a strong pillar for him. Jill's parents wanted her to study in the UK, where they were based. Her older brother was managing their family business, which she was expected to join after completing her postgraduate studies. However, reality turned out differently. She chose to stay back in New York and with her love over everything.

Jill went into her kitchen and opened the fridge. She took out the stewpot of milk, kept it on the slab and opened the kitchen drawer to see if the packet of oats was still there, but couldn't find it. She further opened the next drawer and found a half empty packet. After closing both the drawers, she stood up and kept the packet on the slab next to the stewpot. Arranging the bowl on the slab, she poured some milk in it, added the oats and stirred using the spoon. "I'll keep it basic", she said to herself while stirring continuously. Turning her head towards the basket of fruits, she picked two pomegranates and bent down further to reach the mixer grinder from the large drawer. After preparing the juice, she filled the two glasses, kept them in the tray and stretched her hands to pick the tray. "Laxie, Macy, Momma is coming."

"I have made juice for you both. Taste and tell me how is it", she said in a loud tone while keeping her left leg on the first stair. After giving them the glasses, she came downstairs and picked the bowl of oats. Her home had an open kitchen, with a dining table placed directly in front of it. Next to the dining table was a sofa set, separating the kitchen area from the living room. She folded one leg and sat on the corner of sofa, placed the bowl on the center table and started checking her phone. There was a notification from an unknown number. She clicked on the same to check who it was and tapped on the profile picture but couldn't recognize it. "I hope you are doing okay", it read. She started wondering about the text and thought of texting back. "Mommy, come here", Macy said. "Yes!" Jill replied. "Mommy, where did you keep my teddy bear?" she asked. "In your shelf", Jill replied.

After this slight distraction, she forgot to text back and started scrolling her social media feed while keeping the bowl on her folded lap. She picked the spoon from the bowl and took it slowly near her mouth to eat. Shrugging her shoulders, she left the phone on sofa and kept the empty bowl in the kitchen sink. After opening the gates of the veranda, the cold breeze kept touching her cheeks and feet. "Why am I not wearing the socks today?" she murmured. "Okay, I slept" she continued speaking.

Jill had a habit of sleeping without socks, even when the temperature was as low as 7 degrees. She pulled the jolly chair and placed it near the railing, sat down and folded her legs while stretching them on the railing wall. Her thoughts were not leaving even a tiny space in her head and it felt as if someone wanted to squeeze her tightly and hurt her by playing mind games. "Crazy!" she said while checking the phone. She started to hear some low pitch voices, coming straight from the hall. Macy was standing on the stool and Laxie was standing near it, both of them were searching for something in the kitchen's almirah. "May I know what are you both looking at?" Jill questioned. Macy smiled and replied "Mommy..we", while she was completing her statement, Laxie interrupted in between "Mommy, we are searching for a packet of banana chips which is absolutely healthy and makes body fit". "Ok, but I told you last week that we are running out of chips and will be purchasing them in the month end" replied Jill. "Yeah, Mommy but this is the month end" replied Laxie. "What is it?" asked Jill in a stern voice. "We are searching for the chocolate box that we received this Christmas" replied Macy while winking at Laxie. "Are you saying the truth?" questioned Jill. "This time, absolutely!" replied Laxie. "Ok, come down first. I'll be giving two chocolates to each one of you. Not more than that because excessive chocolate eating can cause what?" asked Jill. "Cavities" replied Laxie. Jill gave two chocolates to Laxie and Macy each.

Curious as she was, Jill picked her phone to check if there was any missed call from Ayra. Unfortunately, there was no sign. She dialed Matt's number to check if he had eaten something or was still in the meeting. He cancelled the call and message flashed on her phone which read "Busy, can't talk now." She texted him back "I want to talk to you. Call me ASAP!"

Jill kept her phone on the dining table, pulled out her laptop from the bag and kept it on her lap. "I should continue writing. Only this could save me from unnecessary things" she said to herself and opened the pad and started typing, "We all are living our lives but in different phases. Things need to be accepted for the way they are and should not be molded according as per the selfish moods", she backspaced and typed again "I am an independent woman. My lifestyle is different", she again backspaced while giving a frowning expression. After taking a deep breath, she started typing again. This time with a clear thought "I am a free soul. I don't want to restrict myself because someone out there wanted me to do something of his own choice. I am on my own and I know where I belong. I respect the boundaries", psst, "There is so much repetition of 'I' in this", She murmured while backspacing everything she had tried to think and write over the past half hour.

"Not the good time", she spoke to herself and pressed sleep button on her laptop. "Not a good day!" she said while keeping the laptop on the chair. "It is definitely better if I spend time with the little ones. Lax, Macy, where are you children?" she called trying to cheer herself up. "Lacy" she repeated. "Coming, Mommy", reply came from the store room. "What are you looking for?" she questioned. "And for god's sake, please turn on the lights" she added. "Searching for our old doll house" replied Laxie. Jill smiled because these girls were always on the go, running around and sometimes causing a commotion. But overall, they were full of love. "I'm lucky" Jill said with gratefulness in her voice.

It was 08:30 on the clock and time to prepare for the dinner. Matt hadn't called back, which sent Jill's calm thoughts spiraling into deep worry. "Long day! I'll sleep early today" she said to herself. "My mood swings have become a thing now, whether it is during the day or evening, same deal", she added. Meanwhile, her phone started to ring. She looked for her phone in the veranda, then in the dining room and by the time she reached to her phone, it stopped ringing. "Daisy?" she said and redialed her number. "Busy, maybe she is calling me back", she muttered. After five minutes, she dialed her number again but it was engaged. She went into the kitchen, opened the fridge and took out two fresh tomatoes and one cauliflower. "We'll eat light food today. Easy digestion, good sleep." She prepared the soup, called Macy and Laxie. All three of them sat on the dining table and drank from their saucers.

"Keep it in the sink", she ordered Macy who stood up leaving the cup and saucer on the dining table mat. Macy ran away, Laxie followed her. "You girls", she said in a demanding tone. "Clean your mess before you leave the place", she added. After keeping everything in the sink, she washed her hands and utensils, kept them on the drying rack and wiped her hands using the hand towel. Turned off the kitchen lights, changed the hall lights, switched to the dim ones and went inside her room.

"Let me check the main door", she said to herself and went near the door, touched the locks and while she was turning around, doorbell rang. She had a smile on her face thinking about Matt. "Ah, this man! Never fails to amaze me" she added and turned around. While she was about to press her left hand on the door knob, the bell started to ring continuously. She felt strange. It had never happened in the 16 years of their marriage.

Matt was a very patient person and there was only one time when he panicked otherwise, he held his emotions very controlled. Jill moved her right leg and bent her body in the right direction towards the window to check who was there. She slowly moved the curtain to peep. There was a sign of sweat on her forehead, making her softly bit inside of her lip. While moving her eyes around, she found no one. Not a soul was visible. She removed the entire curtain just to check clearly. No one was standing outside the door, not in the porch or on the road. She peeped from the door hole to recheck. Her hands slowly unlocked the door and half opened it. After getting a little assurance, she opened the door wide and stepped out. "Who was ringing the bill?" she said in a shaking voice and moved a little forward to check her neighbors. "Is someone playing a prank with us", said Jill and immediately ran inside her home. She locked the doors safely and put back the curtains and covered every ounce of the glass on the wall. After running inside her room, she picked her phone to call Matt. There were seven missed calls on her phone. It was from Matt. She redialed the number, "Hello, Hello. Matt", said Jill. "Babe, what happened? Where were you? Why are you not picking my calls?" Matt's questions came one after the other. "Matt, nothing is good today. I feel a weird energy around me. I am scared. Just then, the doorbell was ringing helplessly and when I went to check it, there was no one. Even when I was driving my car, there was someone in the back", said Jill with a panic in her tone. "Wait..Wait..Who was there? Who?" Matt questioned. "No one was visible" said Jill and started sobbing. "Matt, I am scared" she added. "Jill, babe, I am coming home. Right now. Do not worry", said Matt. "Please come home" said Jill. "Yes, yes, I am coming. Do not disconnect the call", said

Matt. Jill's tears started to fall, making their way through her cheeks to chin. Matt took approximately forty minutes to reach home. He came out of the car, locked it and rang the bell. She unlocked the door and fell into his arms. Matt hugged her tightly, "Sh, I am here. I am here", he said. "Matt, I don't know what is wrong? Why unusual things are happening?" she said. "It's okay. I am right here", said Matt. She looked in his eyes and asked, "But your meeting.." to which he replied "You're important to me and I miss anything for you. Come on, let's go inside."

Both of them entered the house together while Matt's right hand was tightly covering Jill's shoulders. "Do you want some coffee? Shall I make one for you?" said Matt with love in his voice. She made Jill stand in front of her and looked her in the eyes. "Babe, listen to me and this time very-very carefully. Nothing bad has happened and ever will. I am there for and with you. I will always take care of everything and bring comfort whenever you will need it. You are not alone", said Matt while wiping her tears. She closed her eyes and hugged him while her nose was touching his neck. "I love you", she said. "More!" he replied. He told Jill to freshen up while he locked the door and hanged his coat in the hanger. After placing the umbrella in the umbrella stand, he moved it closer to the wall, and checked the curtains hanging near the main door. He then went to the living area, held her hand and took her to the room. "Go and change. You seem tired and it is absolutely necessary for you to sleep on time", he suggested.

Jill went into the washroom, picked the face wash and

squeezed a drop out on her left hand. After splashing some water, she grabbed the hand towel and wiped her face, checked herself in the mirror for more than a minute, applied the cream and went in the changing room to wear her night dress. After five to seven minutes, she came out and sat near the head of the bed. Matt came near her, touched her cheeks with his left thumb and index finger, smiled and told her to lie down. "Someone texted me", Jill said in a hope that Matt will be able to take her words seriously. Matt even did, his actions were proving his care towards her but Jill was not satisfied. She wanted him to take her concern into consideration and give the same attention as it was expected to be given.

Matt was a serious person and responsive one too so his reply came as thought "Who texted?" he questioned. "Only if I knew" replied Jill. "Okay, show me the number." Jill picked the phone, unlocked it and tapped on 'messaging' icon only to show the message history to him. She scrolled for a while but couldn't find the contact number. She exited and again opened the application to make sure she was seeing the right thing. There was no message from any unknown number. Infact the last chat was done with Matt only. She looked into Matt's eyes and said "I am not lying, someone really texted me"

"Okay. I believe you. We will check this tomorrow. It is time to sleep", said Matt. "I am coming in five minutes and till then you will not touch your phone and try to sleep", he continued speaking. Jill nodded while showing her agreement. Matt smiled and went inside the changing room. He grabbed whatever he could find to wear and went outside. "Ahem!"

Matt tried to make his wife pay attention on his presence in the room. "I have been standing here from past five minutes", Matt mocked.

Jill smiled with a heavy heart. He changed the lights of the room, turned on the table lamps. "Is this heater not working? There is so much coldness in our room", said Matt with a smile. "Oh, I have an idea how to keep my lady warm. I will simply sleep next to her, hold her in my arms, give her a forehead kiss and hug her tightly", he continued. "But my lady is in no mood of throwing a smile at me, poor me." Jill smiled and opened her arms, "Come!" she said. Matt snugged in like a baby. "You were supposed to pamper me" she said. "But..I love being pampered by you", he replied.

It took an hour for both of them to sleep, she was laying on the bed and suddenly felt some kind of pressure against her body. She opened her eyes. Matt was sleeping soundlessly on the other side of the bed, covered under the blanket. There was nothing visible near her stomach, not even a pillow. She again closed her eyes and felt the same force as if someone was touching her and this time, too tightly. She sat on the bed and tried waking Matt up. With his half eyes open, he asked "What's wrong?" Jill was blank and agitated, "I felt something, Matt." Matt leaned and looked for the clock, it was 2 AM. He turned towards her and moved his eyes across the room, "Look at me, there's no one in this room except the two of us and only we are sleeping on this bed." She held his hand and said "But Iam not lying. I have not been lying since the morning but everyone thinks that I am insane. " Matt took both her hands in his' and said "I believe on whatever you are saying. The pressure you felt might be the part of your dream. You must have seen something that was not appropriate and ended up having a bad feeling. That's it."

Jill got frustrated listening to the endless explanations. He tried calming her down and said, "Okay, I believe you. Come to me" making her lie comfortably on the bed. Next morning, Jill went to take a bath and as per the routine, woke everyone up and prepared the breakfast. She opened the loaf of bread and while she was holding the knife, she got glimpses of all the mishappenings in front of her eyes. Matt snapped his fingers and asked "What, Madam? Where are my morning kisses?" Meanwhile, Laxie and Macy were giggling and discussing about the last episode of their favorite cartoon show. "Nothing. Have a seat", Jill replied with a smile. She served bread and the butter, poured orange juice in the glass.

Matt knew that Jill was thinking about the things that happened with her. "Hey, are you okay?" he asked while touching her elbow. "I am. Maybe I overthought for no good reasons but now it feels okay" she replied. He smiled and gave her a peck of kiss which made her blush. "Thank you for existing. I don't know what I would have done without you" she said. "Same pinch" he replied.

Before leaving, he hugged her from the backside and whispered in her ears, "I love you." She blushed and for a moment, forgot about all the odd activities. Matt left for his work and girls had their day off so she decided to plan something for them. "Have you brushed your teeth?" asked Jill. "I did it last night", replied Laxie. "Go and brush your teeth first. What is this last day theory and keep the bread from where you took it" ordered Jill. "These girls are impossible to deal with. The logics, god!" Jill said to herself. "I am finishing my work in the kitchen and expect that you both have completed your homework", Jill kept speaking. "Yes, Mommy. We told you to check even" Macy replied.

"Okay, today we will be going to fun zone where you can play, eat, dance, whatever you feel like" said Jill. "No, Mommy! You said swimming", Laxie said with annoyance in her voice. "Yes, but look at the weather, how can you even think of entering into cold water?" questioned Jill while throwing her hands in the air. "Pool areas have hot water facility and they give special treatment to children" said Laxie. "You don't talk like a child to me" replied Jill. "They will definitely focus on the age factor" said Laxie while winking at her mother. "Naughty girls!" said Jill. "Your father will scold us", she continued speaking. "Nothing will happen, Mommy. You remember how we used tubes to swim earlier but now we can deep dive. Skills!" Laxie boasted. "Yes, but we are considering the weather and not going there", replied Jill. "Go and take baths. Don't forget to use the tooth brush while brushing. Fingers won't clean them" she commanded. "Okay, Mommy", said Laxie.

Jill held the packet of bread and picked a slice of it. She opened the box of butter and touched the serrated bread knife to apply butter using it. Meanwhile, her phone started ringing. She kept both the things on the table and went in the direction her phone was ringing. "Where did I leave my phone?" Jill said to herself. She went inside her room to attend the phone call. It was from Ayra. "Oh!" said Jill before answering the call. "Hello?" said Jill. "Hello, Jill" the voice came from the other side. "Yes" said Jill. "Hi, actually tried reaching out to you but you didn't answer my call so I left for a drive with Liam. I even tried calling you sometime later but then again, you didn't answer it", Ayra said. "Yeah, actually I missed it. I even called you too but no one answered", Jill said with a concern in her voice. "You called?" Ayra questioned. "Yes", Jill answered with a little hope of convincing her. "I am not sure if I received any call from your side", Ayra confirmed. "Oh!" this time Jill had confusion in her tone. "Okay, by the way apologies. We planned to go out yesterday but this thought totally slipped off my mind. We can plan it this week", said Jill. "Jill, what are you talking about? We went to the market day before yesterday and I believe we have brought all the necessary items you had on your list" said Ayra. Hearing this, Jill started feeling anxious. "We...did?" asked Jill with a confusion in her tone. She felt as if her hands had left her body and everything started revolving in front of her eyes. She disconnected the call immediately. Ayra called Jill again and screen turned inactive after few seconds.

Jill ran straight into the washroom, stood near the basin, saw herself in the mirror and opened the tap. The water was flowing out of it, and she was continuously staring at the mirror in a hope of finding answers in it. "What is wrong?" she said with a sigh. She put her hands in the flowing water, took water in hand and started splashing water on her face and kept doing this until she was satisfied that everything was on its place and nothing was delusional as it seemed.

Jill came out of the bathroom and dialed Ayra's number. "Hi!" said Ayra. "Hey!" replied Jill trying to avoid what just happened in the past fifteen minutes. "I am sorry, I disconnected the call. Actually, something came on my mind that is why" she continued. "Oh, it's okay" said Jill. "Actually, I called you to confirm if you had my box of bracelet in your paper bag. I couldn't find it here" said Ayra. Jill had no memory of it but she also had no courage left in her to convince Ayra about what she had been experiencing from the past two days. "Okay, I will check it for you" said Jill. Back in Jill's head, the thought was tingling because she couldn't recall anything at that point of time. Last thing she remembered was Matt leaving for his office and she was convincing Laxie and Macy to get ready for the fun zone. "Hello, Hello?" said Ayra. "Yeah, yeah I am listening. I will inform you if I find it" said Jill and disconnected the call. She sat on the floor and the thoughts had a very dim view. She unlocked her phone, tapped on 'phone' icon to check the call logs. There was no call made to Ayra from her side. She kept scrolling and there were only two calls made from her phone which was to Matt and Daisy. No one else!

She clicked on Ayra's contact number, checked the history and there was only a list of incoming calls. She kept her right hand and covered her lips, "I am shocked", said Jill. She leaned her head against the table's leg and kept her phone on the floor. "Mommy" said Macy while sitting on her knees, next to her. "Are you okay?" she added. Meanwhile Laxie sat on the other side, "Mommy", she said. "Children, everything is okay", said Jill. "Can we go now? Look, we are ready just like you said. Come on, let's have our breakfast", said Macy while pulling her left hand to make her stand. "Laxie, Macy, go and arrange your toys. I will put breakfast on the table", said Jill.

"Do it fast. Mommy is super hungry" said Jill while caressing her stomach with hunger. Both the girls started running and headed towards the hall. Jill stood up with all her strength and went near the dining table. She continued preparing the breakfast. "How will I find her bracelet when I don't even remember anything about the shopping?" said Jill to herself. Just when Jill was surmising about all of it, Macy came from the store room and asked "What is this, Mommy?" Jill looked at her and took the bag in her hand. After opening the zip, she found some items tightly adjusted in the space. She kept picking each item one by one and while she was doing it, a pink colored box was visible. After opening the ribbon tied around it, it was a shining rose gold bracelet. It had two diamonds on the ends of its buckle which was actually a surprise for her. She was not able to process the entire thing.

"I don't remember anything and this is so crazy", she said to herself. "Where did you find it? Show me" Jill said to Macy. "Come", Macy held Jill's pinky finger and took her to the store room. She pointed her finger towards the wooden box saying "I found it on the top of it." Jill went near the box and touched it in a hope of finding answers to all her questions. "Okay, call Laxie. We will have breakfast now", Jill said with a half-smile and dialed Ayra's contact number, on the fifth ring she picked up the call. "Hello?" said Jill to which Ayra answered "Hey!" Jill took a pause and said "I found your bracelet. You were right, it was in my bag." Ayra replied with a sincere satisfaction in her voice, "I was so worried. Thank You! Liam will pick it up." "Sure", replied Jill and disconnected the call. She pulled out a dining chair and sat down. Just then, Macy and Laxie arrived.

"I am going to sit next to Mommy", said Laxie. "So am I", Macy asserted. "You can't because there's only one spare chair near her and that's mine", said Laxie. "It's mine" said Macy while stomping her left foot. "It's mine!" said Laxie. Jill was lost in her thoughts and suddenly the bubble busted. "One second, what is this? Why are you two girls fighting?" asked Jill. "She is fighting with me. I simply came and stood here", said Laxie. "Laxie, stop lying. Don't do this. She is your sister", said Jill. "Macy had tears in her eyes because she was really hurt by Laxie's behavior. "Come! Sit on my lap" said Jill. Macy stood at her place like a statue. "Macy, look at me", Jill said. "Apologize to her", she added while looking at Laxie. "I am sorry, Macy" Laxie went near Macy trying to hug her. Macy looked at her and said "Your sorry will only be accepted if you will let me sit near Mommy". "Darling, come to momma", said Jill with her arms opened. Macy went near Jill and touched her cheeks. "Mommy, I want to see you happy and you should never cry even when something bad happens." Jill was not expecting this response from her young girl. "But darling, I am absolutely happy. There is nothing wrong and what made you say this?" asked Jill. "I saw you sad, Mommy. I do not want to see you like this", Macy replied. "I am never sad, see", Jill pointed her index finger towards her lips and smiled. Macy hugged her and Laxie hugged Macy. "We love you!" both the girls said in solidarity. "I love you too", Jill said with her eyes wet. "Okay, now. Jam or butter", Jill asked. "Butter", said Macy. "Jam", said Laxie. Jill gave plates to both and served them one by one. "I was wondering if we can make a snowman", Jill said with a hope of hearing positive answers from both. "I have a muffler to put around its neck", Macy said while looking out of the window.

Sun had not shown its face from past three days and snowflakes were visible all around. "Why are you not wearing your socks?" asked Jill. "Because I like cold floor. It makes me feel good", said Laxie. "And what about you, Macy?" asked Jill while her eyebrows raised and eyes kept searching for an appropriate answer. Macy kept looking at her plate and said "We will have our breads and go out for the snow". Macy tried to change the topic. "Don't act smart you two. Finish this, grab your socks and get ready" said Jill. "I want one more!" said Macy. Jill applied the butter on one bread, placed the plain one on it and gave it to Macy. "You want it too?" asked Jill. Laxie shook her head.

Jill stood up, took her plate to the kitchen. She then opened her fridge, picked two tetra packs of milk, opened them and put paper straws in each. "Take this", she said while handing over one-one pack to each. "Do like I said, I am going to wash myself. Okay?" said Jill. "If anyone calls then answer it and do not fight. I repeat", she continued. Laxie nodded "We will not fight. If someone calls then we will inform the person." Jill smiled and praised the girls. She entered her room, opened the almirah and pulled out a dress from hanger. "It's too cold today. I need my innerwear and snow pants. Oh, I totally forgot to add oak in the furnace" she murmured and walked to the veranda, then the backyard. "I kept the bundle somewhere near the carton", she said while moving the sacks. "Where is it", she asked herself. It was sleeting and she started feeling extremely cold while searching. On moving the third carton, she found a bunch of sticks which were dampened. "Oh", she sighed while picking the bundle up. She opened the gate and kept the oak sticks near the furnace which was about to turn off.

"I will add them in the furnace", she said and went back to her room. "I should inform Matt to bring some more on his way back home. It seems like this was the last bunch we had", said Jill and took the towel in one hand and robe in another. She entered into the bathroom, hanged the garments on the backside of the gate and went near the basin.

Jill had a very compact bathroom, squeezed in a tight space. It was her idea not to make it large because she found it useless, instead she made the store room on the other side of the wall and was happy to have utilized the space in a modern way. For entering the bathroom, it was necessary to cross the changing room since they were attached. After opening the gate, on the right side was a tub covered with a shower curtain and on the left side there was a basin. On the top of that basin, there was a mirror hanged of a definite size and on the right side of it was a stand to put toothbrushes and paste. If gone straight then there was a toilet commode and on the right most corner was a shower panel.

She opened her clothes and entered into the tub. Fortunately, she had already filled it with water and therapeutic oils ten minutes earlier. She put her right leg first and then second, while sitting down, she burnt the scented candles near the faucet. "It's been so long I haven't spent time like this. Self-Love is definitely something", she said to herself.

All the thoughts that were troubling her earlier started to vanish. She eased her body and leaned her head on the border of the tub, making the body below the neck to submerge. She closed her eyes and within fifteen minutes, the bubbles started to form in the water. There were ripples on its surface covering her abdomen making her open eyes when the sound started to become audible. The ripples were forming continuously and it seemed as if someone was placing the finger gently on the surface. She closed and opened her eyes just to confirm what she had witnessed. Trying to keep calm in order to confirm if that effect was an external force and not anything else, she stayed still. The ripples kept forming one after the other, taking her breath away by the shock. She immediately stood in the tub, came out and turned her head to see the water. She moved her right hand inside the hair and left hand was holding the waist. "How is this possible?" she asked herself. Since there were salts and oils in the water, the visibility became low and it turned translucent.

"Is there any worm inside?" she continued speaking to herself.

"Maybe there's some worm. I must have forgot to check the water before entering", she reassured herself by repeating the sentence to herself. She slightly hit the back of her head using her left hand and went ahead to open the drain plug. After taking her towel, she dried off and then unwrapped the robe with the inside facing out. She put her arms through the sleeves and wrapped the robe around her body. After fluffing the robe, she draped it comfortably while looking at the tub. Water was completely drained. She turned on the faucet and picked the handheld showerhead to clean the tub & the bathroom. Later she wore her slippers and came to her room. "Let me check the sticks before getting ready", she said to herself.

Jill made her way towards the furnace. Picking the sticks one by one, she put them on fire. By moving her hands on her hips, she tried to clean her hands. "Laxie, Macy, are you ready?" she questioned while gazing at their room doors from downstairs. Doors of Macy and Laxie's rooms were clearly visible after standing on the first stair. None of them answered. Jill called their names again and started walking upstairs. She kept looking at their room doors and yet again, no one seemed to come out and answer which made her climb the complete stairs. The gates was locked from inside which meant that nobody went there. She came running downstairs and shouted their names from the hall. "Macy, Laxie", she shouted, "Look this is not funny. Where are you?" she said while panting heavily.

She searched for them everywhere but couldn't find any one.

"Doll house?" she said and went to Macy's room but they were not there. Opening the veranda gate, she checked every wall possible and later looked inside the kitchen. There plates were left empty on the table and chairs were visible behind their usual places. She kept running from one place to other and suddenly her eyes were drawn to the half opened door. She looked outside the window which faced the backyard. There were the girls. Laxie was standing and Macy was sitting on her feet. Laxie had one empty sack in her hand and they both were wearing the gloves, trying to do something with the mud.

"Girls!" Jill said. "What are you doing here?" Jill questioned with a millions of bad thoughts chasing her from the past couple of minutes. "We.." said Macy and stopped. "We are searching for the sticks" said Laxie. "For what?" asked Jill. "Fire" said Macy. Jill had no words to describe how she was feeling at that moment. While the girls were worried about the sticks, Jill was in a state of panic. "Wasn't I supposed to know?" asked Jill with her arms folded ahead of her chest. "Mom", said Laxie. "Mom, we called your name but you didn't respond. We even knocked your bathroom door but there was no answer. So we came out ourselves", said Laxie. "I didn't hear you?" asked Jill with a confusion lingering in her eyes.

"Come inside", Jill commanded pointing her index finger towards the door while her right hand was still folded near the chest. "We couldn't find it", said Laxie to her mother. "I know" replied Jill. "There were no sticks and I took the last bunch that we had, inside", Jill said in a very cold voice. Three of them went inside the home and girls started feeling bad to have put their mother in the panic mode. They stood in front of her. "Girls. You have no permission to move outside our home without my permission. If you don't find me, wait for me before you think and start handling everything on your own. This is a last and the final warning", said Jill. "Are you angry?" asked Laxie. "Absolutely! I went crazy searching for you both everywhere" replied Jill. "And how can you forget to put the plates in the sink and throw the cans in the dustbin?" Jill enquired. "We were about to do so" said Macy "But since we saw the fire putting off, we went outside to search the sticks" she added. "Okay, so didn't you both see the sticks near the furnace" asked Jill with the furious expressions on her face. "We did but thought of bringing more" replied Laxie. "Okay. Now go inside and get ready", Jill ordered. The girls went inside their rooms and later, Jill felt guilty about how harsh she was with them. "I should have spoken a bit less", she murmured.

As soon as she closed the door behind her, she went near the furnace and added some sticks. "I had to call Matt", she remembered and picked her phone to dial Matt's number. He answered the phone within thirty seconds and said "Hello?" to which she replied "Hey! Babe I called you to remind about the oak sticks. We have last bunch of them." She took a pause and asked "Hello? Am I audible to you?" to which he answered "Yeah, yea. You are. I will. Was doing something on my phone. Talk to you later". Hearing this, Jill disconnected the call and went into the kitchen to drink some water. She took the jar and poured some water in the glass from it. The jar was half empty. "I should fill this and keep it on the table", she burbled. She held the glass in her left hand and started drinking from it. Meanwhile Laxie and Macy came.

Macy was wearing yellow sweater, a green jacket, beige gloves, warm pants, black boots and a head band where Laxie chose a scarf, rest was same. "What about the socks?" Jill questioned. "We are wearing, Mommy. You can't see them in the boots" said Laxie. "Sure?" Jill asked. "Because it is really-really cold outside. You have just experienced teeth biting weather outside", she continued speaking. "Yes, Mommy. We swear!" said Macy. "Okay" replied Jill. "So are we going to a specific place?" Laxie questioned. "It's a surprise!" said Jill with her palms open & head a little tilted. "Let me wear my jacket and shall I take a muffler?" asked Jill. "Nope! You're okay without it", said Laxie. "Okay", Jill emphasized.

She went inside her room, took out a jacket, wore it and then opened the side drawer of her TV stand to take out her gloves. "I hate wearing them!" she said to herself. "But I have to" she uttered and took an exit from the room. After taking the door keys from the key stand, she directed the girls to stand in the porch outside. "Give me two minutes" she said and locked the door. "What if Liam comes?" she asked herself. "No issues, I'll tell him to visit us later", she added. "Wait, I forgot to bring out the car keys", she said in an apologetic tone. "We will wait" said Macy while looking at Laxie.

Jill went inside hurriedly, kept the bag on the side table and started searching the car keys. Oh, I hung them on the wall.

She turned around and went near the key stand. "What kind of person am I? Took the door keys and left the car ones" she kept talking to herself. After picking the keys, she latched the door and went outside. Pressed the unlock button by touching the padlock icon on the key fob. There was a sound of click and lights flashed. "Get inside", Jill said. "Laxie, can I sit in the passenger seat?" Macy questioned. Laxie placed her finger near the forehead and started tapping it lightly. "Hm, Let me think", she said.

For the time being, Jill sat inside and waved her hands. She pressed the button located on the center console in order to pull the window down. "Girls!" she exclaimed. "Okay, you can sit" said Laxie while she opened the door on the backseat and sat inside. Macy smiled with an excitement and sat beside her mother. "I don't know what I will do without you two and my Matt", Jill said while looking at the girls. "You'll miss us", Laxie said. "Won't you?" asked Jill. Laxie smiled.

She turned on the car and looked in the mirror to take a reverse. When the car was aligned with the road, she changed the gear and the car started moving forward. "Today, we will try Thai food", said Jill. "What is it?" asked Macy. "Have we ever tasted it in the past?" asked Laxie. "I said try which means it is going to be our first time" said Jill. "What if we don't like it?" asked Laxie. "We can't predict", said Jill while giving a look. "How much time would we take to reach our surprise destination?" asked Laxie while looking out of the window. Jill turned on her wipers to remove the waters droplets from the windshield. "Forty five minutes, approximately" said Jill. "I'd love it!" said Macy.

Macy loved to go on drives especially on the windy days. She often called herself as "A free bird". Laxie on the other hand wanted everything to be quick. She never liked waiting and hated the long journeys. Laxie rolled her eyes and kept her hand near her heart "I hope we reach early." Jill smiled knowing the girls will enjoy the destination. "Talking of the surprise destination, I...I am very much excited to see you on the snow ground", said Jill. The girls started jumping on their seats with excitement. "I will make a snowman. I will name him 'Soft'." "Is that even a name?" asked Jill. "No. But yes!" said Macy. "I will throw snow balls on you", said Laxie to Macy. "I will make an igloo", said Macy. "I will make it too" Laxie remarked.

"Oh no! I forgot to message my Boss", Jill said to herself. She told Macy to take her purse and search for the phone. After slowing down her car, she checked the side mirrors & applied the parking brake. Car stopped with the dipper on. "Give me", she said to Macy and unlocked her phone to open Jacob's chat. She started typing "Boss, I am outside home and won't be working today. Please pin me on the tasks, I will try and finish them whenever I'll get time." After hitting 'send', she handed over the phone back to Macy and started driving again. "Girls, we are almost there. Embrace the journey for now", Jill said.

After a while, there was a board visible which said 'Ski Area'. Laxie read it and started jumping on her seat with excitement. "Are we going skiing?" asked Laxie. "Of course!" said Jill. She moved her car in the right direction and after driving for a minute, parking board was clearly visible. "Get out of the car and stand near the pole. Do not move from there. I am coming", Jill said. "Okay!" both the girls moved out of the car, feeling exhilarated.

"Iam going to try green trails", said Macy. "I know how to do it. I will teach you", said Laxie. While the girls were chit chatting, Jill was trying her best to park the car aligning with the others. Her hands were on the steering and suddenly she heard as if someone was laughing. She looked back to check if someone was there. The energy was so strong that it felt as if her throat was choking. Hesitating, Jill moved rear view mirror in order to check the atmosphere around the backseat. The sweat droplets started to fall from her forehead, making their way through the tip of the nose. "Why am I sweating?" she asked herself pretending that everything was normal around her. She cleaned her cheeks using the right hand while the left hand rested on the steering. "Nothing! Still nothing!" she said. "As if I was expecting someone", she added after crosschecking. She turned to check the corners of the back seat but just like before, there was absolutely nothing.

She saw the girls standing and waving towards her, "I should go, now. This mess can wait", she said while collecting the strength in her voice. It seemed as if she had embraced the strange energies and was letting her thoughts drift away with a sigh. "Like Matt said, if I will think about such petty things, I won't be able to move forward. Plus, everything is in my head", Jill said after exhaling a long breath. After opening the car gate, she moved her left foot out while her focus was on the phone and the bag. "It is terribly cold!" she said to herself while locking the car behind.

Jill crossed the passage to reach near the girls. "Shall we go?" she asked. "We are ready!" Macy replied. "Mommy, Am I allowed to do skiing without a trainer?" asked Laxie. "Who said we will be hiring a trainer? This is your day, you can enjoy everything but with safety", answered Jill. The moment these words left her mouth, the girls started jumping and the happiness was evident on their faces. "Seems like you're having fun with me", said Jill. "So, now my question is, whom do you love the most? Me or Dad?" asked Jill with a hope of hearing her name before her husband's. "Both", replied Laxie with a smile. Jill expected the same answer and smiled post hearing that. "We will always love you, no matter what" said Macy. "And we won't ever leave you alone", said Laxie. "My angels" replied Jill while holding their hands.

It was a long track before the actual outing spot started. There was a huge gate marking the entry and on the right side, there was something written on the marble. On getting closer, Jill read, "SKII FUN" and entered the gate. After walking eight to ten steps, there was a dome shaped counter available. Macy and Laxie started talking about the snow. "Look there!" said Macy. She pointed her fingers in the left direction and a steep slope was vaguely visible. "Wow!" Laxie exclaimed. "Let's go near it", she added. "Mom will scold us", said Macy.

While the girls were chit chatting, Jill stood near the counter. There was no body to attend her there. "Hey!" Jill called but even after waiting for more than fifteen minutes, nobody replied. Few people were sitting in the waiting area, so she walked to them and asked "Hey, Can you please tell me about the ski tickets?" A woman sitting on the iron bench looked at her and said, "We are waiting for the tickets only. The woman from the counter has not come yet and guard told us to wait here." Jill heard the words and her eyes started searching for the girls. "Come here", Jill said. Laxie and Macy came running to her and said "Yes, Mommy". Jill kneeled down and said "The woman responsible for providing the ski tickets is not available. The guard has informed these people to wait here until she comes. So it will take slightly more time but I promise, we will have ski session today". Laxie's face dropped after hearing her mother's words. "But?" Macy said and stopped immediately. "Okay!" said Laxie with the disappointment in her voice. "Can we stall around till then?" asked Laxie. "Yes but don't go far", replied Jill with the firmness in her voice. "Never", said Macy and both the girls held each other's hand and took an exit from the dome.

Jill folded her hands around her chest and started strolling. An hour passed and suddenly she saw a woman standing near the counter post. The people started forming the queue according to the sequence of arriving to the place. "I came before you", said a man to Jill. "Sure", she replied and created a space for him to stand ahead her. After ten minutes, Jill's chance came. "How much?" she questioned. The woman smiled and said "For adults, the price is 65 Dollars and for children under twelve, it is 35 Dollars." "Actually, I am buying the tickets for my children so what will be the cost. Plus, I don't want to ski" said Jill. "But there are going to be the visiting charges", said the woman while her eyebrows raised. "Okay, how much?" questioned Jill. "Visiting charges are 15 Dollars and this won't include ski and other sports", replied the woman. "No worries, two tickets for the children and one for a visit", said Jill. "May I know the age of you children?" the woman questioned while writing something on her register. "They are somewhere around ten", replied Jill. "Twins", she added. "Okay, your total amount is 85 Dollars. Only cash accepted, no cards", said the woman. Jill unzipped her purse, counted the money and handed over to the woman. The woman started counting back just for the reassurance and kept the money in the drawer. She noted down the details and issued three tickets to her. "Make sure you submit this visiting ticket on the counter No 3 and show it to the guard while entering the snow area", said the woman. "Okay!" replied Jill. "Have a great day", said the woman with a smile. Jill took the tickets in her left hand and wrapped her right palm around the chain of her bag.

"Macy, Laxie", Jill said in a clear voice. "Macy", Jill said again. There was no reply. "I told these girls not to go far", said Jill. As Jill covered some distance, she found the girls sitting on the bench under the shed, deeply involved in their conversation. Jill walked and stopped near them. Macy looked upwards to ask "Are we having the tickets now?" "Definitely. You didn't hear me?" asked Jill. "You called our names?" asked Laxie. "Yes", Jill's expressions were firm and voice, bold. "I was looking for you", said Jill. "Sorry, Mommy but we swear we didn't hear you", said Macy. "No problem. Now get up, we are going for a fun ride", said Jill. "Ride? No Mom, no more. We came this far to go on a ride again?" Laxie questioned. "Ride means spree. We are going to have fun", said Jill.

Laxie looked at her with a confusion but was happy imagining the bigger picture. "Yayaye!" replied Macy with an excitement in her voice. "Mommy, will they be providing us the boots?" Laxie questioned. "Yes", replied Jill. "Mommy, can we take ice cream sticks from the bar?" asked Macy. "No", replied Jill. "Mommy, are you going to come along too?" asked Laxie. "I will sit on the bench, watch you play and click pictures", said Jill. "Mommy, are we going to come here every week?" asked Macy. "No, because Mommy doesn't get day offs like this. Since today was a special day, that's why", said Jill. "Mommy, what's so special today?" asked Laxie. "Today is my birthday", said Jill. "Wait, what? But your birthday is on 2nd January", said Laxie with a surprise in her tone. "That is not original but in the documents", said Jill. "What does that even mean?" asked Macy. "It means that in my official documents, 2nd January is my birthdate but in reality, it is today", said Jill.

That was an eye opening reveal for Macy and Laxie. Seeing them, Jill said "You are too young to understand this, children". While they were busy in themselves, Laxie saw the guard. "I think we have reached" to which Jill replied "This is the first checkpoint, we're almost there." "Tickets?" asked the guard. Jill showed the tickets to him. He stamped the passes and showed the path to move ahead. "They give green signals too", said Macy. "Obviously", said Laxie. "Seems as if you have been here a lot", said Macy. "Have I ever gone anywhere without you?" asked Laxie. "Then how do you know so much about it?" asked Macy. "I know everything" replied Laxie.

As the second check point came, Jill showed the tickets to person standing behind the table in the tent. He had covered almost every part of his body except the face. "It's really cold, Sir", said Jill to show her friendly presence. "Absolutely", replied the man while looking at the stamps on the tickets. "You're with?" questioned the man with his eyebrows raised and mouth half opened, expecting an answer. "With my twin daughters", replied Jill. "Do you need a trainer?" asked the man. Jill would have asked for the same but Laxie requested to do things alone so she denied saying "No, Sir. My girl is an expert as per say". The man shrugged his shoulders and said "There's only one visiting pass and we don't provide the suit and glasses on the same. Do you wish to buy it?" to which Jill replied "No, Sir. Only two suits, snow goggles and sticks." The man handed over the set to her and said "Have a great time, Ma'am".

Jill made the girls ready in the suit, gave them the sticks and told them to wear the ski goggles. "I'm sitting here, you can do as you wish but do not disturb the people and be safe", she said. "We have planned everything and will not give a chance of getting a scolding from you, Mommy", said Laxie. "Okay, go now!" Jill said while waving her hands towards them and gave a flying kiss.

"Yuhuu!" screamed Laxie with an excitement. She started practicing the gliding on a flat terrain to get a feel for the skis. "Macy, look at me now. Do as I say, you'll be able to learn and understand quickly", directed Laxie. "But, what if I fall?" asked Macy. "Stand again and start the process", said Laxie. While saying this, she made a pizza position to slow down and stop. "See, you can keep your tips close together and the tails apart. This helps you control your speed and stop. When you will gain confidence, work on bringing your skis parallel to each other for smooth turns", Laxie added.

Macy started trying as Laxie instructed, "Is this correct?" Laxie replied "No, make space between your legs like this. You have to keep your tips straight and space between the legs should be definite". "What happened?" asked Laxie. "Nothing", Macy replied while the pressure was visible on her face.

Both the girls were having fun and Jill was looking at them. Her phone started ringing and hands were continuously shivering while she removed her glove from left hand. "Maybe, it is Matt calling", she said to herself while removing the buckle and unzipping the purse. She searched for her phone and looked at the screen. It was from an unknown number. "Unrecognizable!" said Jill. She took a second and answered the call. "Hello?" said Jill while looking at the girls playing in front of her eyes. There was silence on the other side of the phone. "Hello?" she repeated. There was no word from the other side. "Hello?" she said for the third time but there was no response. "Hello? I think you're not audible", Jill said while keeping her finger in one ear in hope of listening clearly. There was pin drop silence and suddenly phone was disconnected. "I don't know. Shall I call back?" she asked herself and while she was thinking this, there was a beep sound on her phone. "How are you?" it read. This message was from the same number she earlier received a call. "Who is it?" Jill typed and sent after re-reading the message thrice. She started tapping on the back side of her phone using her index finger. "What does this message mean?" she said to herself while reading the message again and again.

Jill typed again "Who are you?" and locked her phone. After few seconds, she unlocked her phone to check if there was any message but no response. "Someone must have called me by mistake. But what does that text mean?" Jill said to herself and called back on the same number. After few rings, the call got disconnected and there was no answer. She checked for the voicemail setup and tapped on the icon. "Hey, I have received a call and text from your number. May I know who this is?" Jill said.

The girls came running towards Jill and said "Mommy, let's make a snowman", said Macy. "No, we will make a snow woman", said Laxie. "We can make both but darling, I'm not allowed to do so. I have only visiting pass, you can go and make it", said Jill. "Go!" Jill said while patting their backs. "Where is your muffler?" asked Laxie. "I kept it in the bag. Mommy, where's the muffler?" asked Macy from a distance. "I cannot hear you. What?" asked Jill while keeping her hand over her ear. Macy came near Jill and said "Mommy, my muffler" to which Jill questioned "Where is it?" Macy kept looking at her mom before saying "I gave you before entering the snow area". "You gave?" asked Jill. "Yes", replied Macy while touching her bag. "You kept it in this", Macy added. "But the bag is too small to keep a scarf inside", said Jill. "Then you must have kept it in another bag", said Macy. Jill searched for the muffler inside her bag and then the carry bag but there was no sign of it. "Ahem" Jill said while clearing her throat. "Someone has the muffler around her neck", said Jill.

Macy looked down and said "Oh!" and she removed it from her neck and ran towards Laxie. "Laxie, don't start without me", said Macy. "I have already started; please come quickly and fix it", shouted Laxie while making a ball of snow using both her hands. "We have to dig the snow using our hands since there's no shovel here", said Laxie. "Let me gather the snow", said Macy "and then it will be easy for both of us to use it", she added. "Macy, pass me that stick", said Laxie. "Where is it?" asked Macy. "Near your left knee" said Laxie while her one hand was out to take it.

Macy moved her neck, took the stick and gave it to Laxie while saying "Do not use it completely. I too need it" Laxie looked at Macy and said "I am not putting it inside, it's just for the hole in the face. "Do it carefully, stack the snow balls on top of each other. Keep the largest one in bottom then the medium one and smallest one on the top", said Laxie. "For the eyes, I will make a hole, but what to put inside of it?" asked Laxie. "Take a stone", said Macy.

"From where will I get the stone?" asked Laxie while touching her waist. "Let's leave everything here and search for a stone. What else do we need?" asked Macy. "Um, something for a nose, sticks and a few branches", replied Laxie. "We already have a scarf as the head gear", she added. "Okay, let's go", Macy stood up and held Laxie's left hand with her right. "Shall we inform Mommy", asked Macy. "No, we ain't going far. Just a few steps", said Laxie. They both looked at Jill's side while she was looking at her phone.

After a few minutes, both of them went near their snow structures with the bunch of sticks and branches in their hands. "We have to make it the best", said Laxie. "Of course!" replied Macy and both of them started working on their structures. "Mommy" shouted Laxie while waving her hands in the air. "Mommy", said Macy. Jill looked at the girls and kept her phone in the bag. "Shall I?" Jill asked. She walked a few steps and stood next to the girls. "Oh my god!" Jill exclaimed. "This is amazing", she added. There were two beautiful snow structures in front of her. "A snowman and a snowwoman", Laxie said. "And they are married", Macy explained. "Okay", Jill emphasized on the word. "Let me click your picture", she continued speaking. Macy touched the sticks of their hands and both the girls stood next to the snow structures. Jill smiled and said "Say cheese!" while clicking the picture. She then showed it to them saying "Girls! Look how beautiful this capture is". Laxie and Macy started jumping in joy. "Mom, we are so happy. We had so much fun", said Laxie. "Absolutely! Thank you, Mommy", said Macy. Happiness was visible on Jill's face, "I'm glad that you enjoyed. Now, shall we go?" she asked. "No, Mom", Laxie asserted. "It's time baby. We will get late and dad will be home. It won't be nice if he waits outside in this weather. We have the door keys", said Jill in a convincing voice. "Okay", said Macy while making an eye contact with her sister. "Take all your stuff", said Jill. Laxie removed the muffler from her snow man and said "Bye, snowy. We will meet soon." Jill smiled and said "You got attached to it. I wish we could take them but it isn't practically possible." Laxie and Macy looked at their snow structures and said "Bye! Don't miss us much."

Jill held their fingers and all three of them headed towards their car. "We parked our car in L1. Search for it" said Jill. "K11, K12, K13, L1, Here it is", said Macy while pointing towards their car. Jill unlocked it using her keys and said "Get inside.

Keep my purse on the back seat and don't touch the phone". Laxie opened the car door and took a seat in the back, while the other two sat on the front seats. Jill reversed her car and as they took an exit from the parking area, snowflakes were noticeable. "Macy, what's the time", asked Jill. "Mommy, Laxie has your purse. Laxie, what is the time?" asked Macy. "You told me not to touch the phone but it is 17:04 by the way", Laxie replied. "You, girl. We will take approximately one hour to reach home since it is snowing and we might find a traffic" said Jill.

"Mommy, turn on the heater" Laxie said while shivering. The tiny muscles at the base of her hair follicles contracted, causing the hair to stand up. She could feel that under her jacket. "Yes, Mommy. It's too cold" said Macy. Jill adjusted the car's temperature and questioned "Now, is it alright?" Laxie nodded her head while her teeth kept chattering. "It will be okay in a while. Surprising how you didn't feel an ounce of cold while playing with snow", Jill said while looking in the rear view mirror. "Because we were having fun and now it's a car trip, again", Laxie replied. Jill smiled and concentrated on the road. After driving for few miles, she slowed down the speed of her car. "Told you, we'll find traffic."

They stayed stuck in traffic for more than half an hour. She kept on tapping her finger on the steering and honking wherever it was needed to showcase her urgency to leave the place. "How much time is it going to take, Mommy?" asked Laxie. "Daddy is about to arrive", said Macy. "I know but I can't help it", said Jill while turning on the windshield. "It is snowing like there's no tomorrow, I hope it clears soon and we don't run out of fuel", said Jill.

After a few minutes, traffic seemed to clear. There was heavy snow in past one hour and tree limbs fell on utility lines causing that havoc. As the car in front of her started moving, Jill thanked god "We are going home." Laxie and Jill gave a high five to each other, embarking their mini celebration. "I am going to play with my doll", said Macy. "I need to change her clothes since it is so much cold out there" she added. "Since when dolls have started feeling anything?" asked Laxie. Macy looked at her as if she was saying something alien. "Doll is a person too. It feel things", said Macy. "Then why do you use 'It' to define the person?" asked Laxie while emphasizing more on the word 'person'. "Well 'It' can be used for the animals and for your kind information, they are alive", replied Macy while looking outside the window to ignore Laxie's face.

"Will you two stop?" Jill questioned. We are about to reach home and god, we had a great day. Talk about how much you enjoyed this day, discuss good things. Why do you keep indulging in petty fights?" she said while looking at Macy and partially at Laxie. "Mommy, can we take a day off tomorrow?" asked Laxie. "I told you darling, I can't afford to take one more off. You know, my boss will scold me for dodging his calls and not working today", replied Jill. "Mommy, I'm saying can we both, Laxie and Macy take the day off?" Laxie said while pointing the index finger towards herself.

"Do you really think I'll leave you both alone at home?" asked Jill. "Absolutely not but you can call Aunt Mary to stay with us" replied Laxie. "Now, who is Aunty Mary?" asked Jill while rolling her eyes. "She is our mentor, our teacher and helper", replied Laxie while her eyes lit up. "Have I met her? Jill questioned and immediately applied the brakes. A man came in front of her car and she couldn't spot him from a distance. She rolled the window down and apologized to him. "Hey, I am sorry", she said. The man waved his hand towards her showing the sign of forgiveness and the acceptance of her apology. "Now, don't talk and let me concentrate", said Jill.

It wasn't much time since Jill started driving. "Mommy, when did you learn driving?" Macy questioned. "When I turned 22, my daddy gifted me a car. Just after then, I joined driving school and got a chance to use my skills", said Jill while her eyes were glued on the road. "And when did Daddy learn it?" asked Laxie. "When you were born", said Jill. Daddy was not familiar with cars and driving until you both came into our lives. He wanted to caress every moment with you and that's why wanted to protect you from the start."

"So, how is this related to car driving?" asked Laxie. "You'll understand when you will get old. For now, just know that he is a better driver than I am even though I started learning before him", said Jill with a little laughter in her voice. "Mommy, I have one more question", said Laxie. "No more questions now", replied Jill. "Now, we will talk after we reach home", she added.

"Mommy, how long will it take to reach home?" asked Laxie. "Just five minutes", replied Jill. "How can you forget the routes? We travel from this lane almost every day", said Macy while scolding Laxie. "So, what? I am never interested in looking out of the windows. It's your job", said Laxie. "Shh", said Jill while keeping her left finger on her lips.

Jill applied the car brakes and the girls jumped out if it. "Slowly!' Jill warned. Laxie waved towards her mother and shut the door behind her. Both the girls started running, hoping to touch the main door of the house, first. "You'll fall. Slow down" said Jill while locking the car. "Can you at least stop for the one who is going to open the gate for you?" she asked while walking. "Mommy, come fast. It's snowing and I want to enter the home first", said Laxie. "Coming!" said Jill while showing her palm sign to them. She stood near the girls and put her hand in the purse.

Jill opened the main door and girls started pushing the door to enter first. "Yayyae! I won" said Macy. "No, you didn't. I touched the door first so technically I entered first", replied Laxie. "Will you stop giving wrong logics? We decided the winning factor for the one who is going to enter the home first", said Macy. While the girls were arguing, Jill locked the door back and went near the furnace to check the logs.

"I should call Matt again so he don't forget to bring the sticks", said Jill to herself. She kept the purse on the table, hanged the keys on the hook and took her phone in her hands. She dialed Matt's number, but her eyes were suddenly drawn to an unknown number. "Don't know who this person was but he or maybe she hasn't given a call back", said Jill before dialling Matt's number. "Call not reachable", it said. She again tapped on the phone icon, Matt answered after few rings and said 'H-ell-lo'. Matt's voice kept breaking for the next few seconds. "Hello?" Jill said. There was a continuous buffering sound. "Matt? Am I audible to you?" asked Jill. She disconnected the call and redialled the number. "Hello?" Matt answered. "Jill, can you hear me?" he added. Before Jill could respond, Matt's questions came one after the other. "Hello?" said Jill. Matt sighed and replied "Thank god you are safe". She was confused after hearing that statement, "What does that mean?" she said. "I was calling you since noon but your phone was not reachable", he replied. "But I didn't receive any notification from your side", she answered. "Okay, leave it. I wanted to remind you about the sticks. Please don't forget to bring them. I might have called you several times and this is very irritating..I know..I know..", she kept explaining. "But now worries..If we do not stock them, we'll end up sleeping in cold", she added.

"I am leaving the office now and will definitely collect them on my way. Anything else, Madam?" asked Matt. "No, just come home", said Jill while moving her right hand around her neck. "And what can I make for you in dinner?" asked Jill. "Can I cook dinner for you, today?" asked Matt. Jill started blushing because no matter what happened in their lives, he never missed a chance to surprise her. "No, I will make it for you", said Jill while trying to hide her smile as if Matt could see it through the phone. "If woman smiles then it means she's in love", said Matt while picking up his bag and putting the strap on his right shoulder.

"I'm taking an exit, will be there in an hour", said Matt. "Okay", Jill replied while looking at the clock. It was 09:05 P.M. Jill kept her phone on the centre table and started arranging things. "Macy, take your doll from here and keep it back on the place", Jill ordered. "No, Mommy. I'm still playing", replied Macy from her room. Jill looked upwards while standing near the staircase. "Take this in your room and play", she repeated.

Meanwhile Laxie came while rubbing her eyes and said "Mommy, I want to sleep. Can I have my dinner now?" Jill touched her cheeks and replied "Of course but Mommy will take some time to prepare it. Can you wait for fifteen minutes?" Laxie looked her in the eyes and replied "Can I have tomato soup? It's really cold and I want to have something hot for now." "Sure, replied Jill. "Sit here", she added while pulling out the chair of dining table. Laxie sat on the chair and kept her left hand on the table, making her chin rest on it. "Macy, sissy is taking tomato soup in her dinner, do you want the same?" Jill questioned. "Macy, are you listening?" Jill came in the hall to sound better. "Coming, Mommy", Macy replied while running down the stairs. "Do not run", you'll get yourself hurt", warned Jill.

"Mommy, can you make vegetable soup for me?" asked Macy. Jill took a long breath and replied "Okay, Madam. Tomato one for you and vegetable one for you. Anything else?" Laxie took a pause and said "Krutones?" to which Jill replied "I'm afraid that we are running out of them." Macy moved near the kitchen slab and said "We'll settle without Krutones but do not forget our super healthy and tasty cream." Jill kept both her hands around her waist and answered "Sure, Ma'am. Now, go and change your dresses and why are you still wearing those dirty boots?"

Laxie climbed the stairs, Macy followed her back and asked "Hey, are you ok?" Laxie nodded her head without saying anything. Macy held her left elbow and said "But you don't seem that way. Is there anything?" Laxie was too tired to continue the conversation but she still closed it by saying "No." Macy never saw Laxing behaving like this. She was always ready to fight on almost anything but that day, Laxie didn't even ask for the cream. "Don't run your horses, I am too tired to even change my clothes. Mommy told me to have something before going to bed, that's why I suggested her for the soup", Laxie said in a shriek voice. "Do you need my help?" asked Macy while holding her doll in her arms. "No, I will handle. You keep your doll", replied Laxie. Both of them were standing near the wall which was separating their rooms. Jill was watching both of them. They came downstairs after twenty minutes and sat on the chairs of the dining table. "Here is your soup and yours too", Jill said while keeping their soup cups on the table. "Keep your placemats before you start drinking it", she added.

Macy stood and shifted towards her right and grabbed two placemats. "Take this", said Macy while handing over one placemat to Laxie. Both of them were sitting in front of each other. "And do not spill. I have changed the table cover in the morning. Take your time and drink slowly", said Jill. She moved back to the kitchen and started watching the tomatoes. She opened the tap and kept the tumbler under the water, submerged the tomatoes. "Today I will be making Black bean burgers for your daddy", said Jill.

The moment Macy heard her mom say this, she looked up and said "Can I have one too?" Jill smiled and asked "Will you be having any space left in your small tummy after drinking the soup?" Macy moved out of the chair and came near her mother to say "No worries, I'll compromise some soup for the burger." Jill sat on her knees and said, "We should never waste our food. There are so many people out there who do not have the privilege to eat it. We should always and always finish the food on our plates before leaving the table." Macy looked down and replied "Okay, Mommy."

When Macy turned to move, Jill said "But that doesn't mean you can't have your burger, sweety" hearing which Macy jumped and thanked her mother. Jill stood up and asked Laxie, "Will you be interested in eating the burger?" Laxie was about to complete her bowl, so she denied. "I think I'm full", she said. Keeping the bowl on the table, she took out the napkin from her lap and cleaned her lips using its corner. She left the napkin near the bowl, stood up and said "Goodnight, Mommy."

Jill stopped Laxie and said "At least wash your mouth, darling. Don't forget to use your tooth brush before hitting the bed. Okay?" She emphasised more on the last word. Laxie smiled and replied with a yes, while receiving a good night kiss from her mother on the cheeks. "Goodnight Macy", said Laxie while she was holding the railing of the stairs. "Goody nighty", replied Macy while taking a sip of her soup.

Jill went back in the kitchen and opened the packet of burger buns. She later opened the refrigerator and picked the few leaves of lettuce, the packet of ketchup and mayonnaise, kept all three items on the slab and took the tomatoes out of the water. Moving on the side, she kept knife and board near the microwave. She then took a bowl from her crockery cabinet and started adding items in it. "Some salt, black pepper, seasonings, mashed potatoes", she said to herself while mixing the items. Using the potato masher, she left some chunks for the tender texture. In another bowl, she mixed some mashed black beans, breadcrumbs, egg, minced garlic, chili powder and cumin. "Oh, god! I forgot to chop tomatoes and onions", she said while tapping her forehead.

Taking the knife, she carefully sliced thin layers of tomatoes and onions. Heating olive oil in a skillet over medium heat, she started cooking the patties made from the potatoes and added mixture for about 4-5 minutes on each side until they were golden brown and crispy on the outside. She opened the packet of cheese, added a slice on top of each patty during the last minute of cooking to melt. While the patties were cooking, she spread a thin layer of butter on the cut sides of the bun while toasting them in a separate pan.

She then spread the prepared condiments on the bottom half of each bun, placed the cooked veggie patty on the bun, and added some lettuce, tomatoes, pickle, onion and a slice of fresh cheese. Later, covered the material with other half of the bun. "Voila!" she exclaimed. "Macy, here is your burger. Have it", she said while keeping the plate on the table and making a smiley face on the top of bun using the ketchup. "Coming, Mommy", said Macy. "But I won't be able to eat it full, I already had my share of soup so could you please cut it in half?" asked Macy.

"Okay, give it to me", said Jill and went back into the kitchen. She took the knife and separated two pieces, kept one in the common plate and left the other in Macy's plate. "Darling, do you feel like having French fries? I have some more peeled potatoes which I'm thinking of...." She took a pause "frying", Jill said. Macy nodded her head in agreement and sat on the chair. Jill kept the plate having half burger bun on the dining table. "Yum!" said Macy. "I wish Laxie too had eaten this", she added while looking at the Laxie's bedroom door. Meanwhile Jill quickly fried the potatoes and sprinkled the salt on them. "Take!" said Jill while keeping the plate near her hands. "Thank you for the amazing day, Mommy", said Macy. "I am happy that you had a good time", said Jill.

Macy and Laxie have always loved the idea of including continentals in their food. Take it from Croissant to french onion soup to garlic mashed potatoes with a touch of American cuisine (Burgers). Both the girls never missed a chance of eating the food of their choices but that time, Laxie seemed uninterested which kept bothering Jill and Macy.

Jill stayed in the kitchen and prepared few more patties to stay prepared before Matt comes. In the meantime, Macy finished her plate, kept it near the sink and went back in the hall. "Baby, it's late now. Go back to your room and get inside the blanket. It's cold and you have to go to school tomorrow", she instructed.

Macy picked her toys and went inside her room followed by Jill. She entered the Laxie's room where she found her lying diagonally on the bed. "This girl", said Jill while fixing her position. She then opened her blanket and tucked in around the sides and foot of the bed to keep it in place and create a cozy, secure feeling. Fixing the curtains, Jill turned off the lights from the left side of the wall and closed the door of her room. She then went into Macy's room, saw her sitting on the bed and talking to herself. "Macy, you are supposed to sleep now. We had a long day. Come on, get inside your blanket", said Jill while picking the toys from the floor and keeping them in the basket.

Macy stood on the corner of the bed, tried to pull her blanket and failed. "Mommy, this is too heavy", she said. "Lie on the bed, I will do it for you. Have you cleaned your teeth?" asked Jill. "Yes", said Macy while showing her upper and lower teeth. "Hm, Okay. If you need water then you can have it", said Jill while pointing towards the jar of water near her bedside.

She then tucked Macy inside her blanket, adjusted the curtains, turned on the mosquito mat machine and switched off the lights. "Goodnight love", said Jill to which Macy replied

"Goody Nighty". Jill smiled and closed her door, turned off the stair lights and came downstairs. She then checked the time and it was fifteen minutes past ten. "Matty is late", she said to herself while putting her hands around the waist. She removed the curtain hanging near the main door to check if there was a car parked outside. "I think I should call him", she picked her phone. Suddenly, her doorbell started to ring. Using her peep hole, she tried to find if Matt was standing outside it and she was right, her husband was ringing the doorbell.

She opened the door immediately, took the bag from his hands and asked "Hey, where is your car? And why are you drenched?" Matt moved his hands around his shoulders, trying to remove the water droplets. "My car broke few meters back and as soon as I left the car, it started raining", saying this Matt moved inside the house. She looked outside and then shut the door back. "Stand near the furnace, I am bringing your clothes", she said with a stressed look visible on her face and ran inside the room to bring a comfy pair of dress in her hands. "Go and change fast. You'll catch cold otherwise", she said while patting his back.

After some time passed, Matt came outside and checked the furnace. "We are running out of the sticks and I didn't get a chance to stop by the shop. I am sorry", he said with a guilt in his tone. "Let me ask Mrs Derek if she could help us by any means", she said while dialling a number on her phone. He went into his room to keep his laptop. "No more work. We will be having our dinner first", she said while moving her index finger in the air. "Definitely, Madam", he replied.

"Hello Mrs Derek?" said Jill. "Hey!" exclaimed Mrs Derek. "Hi, actually I made you this call to ask for the sticks to put in the furnace. Matt was supposed to bring them but his car broke down", said Jill with a mild smile. "Um, we must be having. I'm coming outside in 5" said Mrs Derek and disconnected the call. Mrs Derek lived three houses away from Jill's place. She lived with her husband, both in their 50s and their children settled in Britain seven years ago.

Jill faced Matt and said "She is having some. I will take them and come back real quick". Saying this, she went outside the door and stood near the pole present in front of their home. **A few minutes later, she saw a woman approaching her, holding an umbrella and a paper bag**. "Hi", said Jill while giving a side hug to Mrs Derek. "Hello, How are you?" she replied. "Absolutely fine", said Jill. "Actually we are running out of the sticks and believe me, this is the first time I missed to notice the availability. Otherwise I wouldn't have made you walk this far", said Jill while keeping her hand on her heart. "Don't worry about it. Take these. I gotta go now", said Mrs Derek and gave a sweet smile to her. "Thank you again", said Jill and headed back to her home.

"Jill, have you seen today's newspaper. There was a column we discussed in our office today and I think I need to read it in detail", said Matt. "All the work post dinner", she replied while keeping the bag of sticks near the furnace and put some out of them in the fire. "I am so happy we are going to have candlelight dinner today", Jill said while softly clapping her hands. "Candlelight dinner?" Matt questioned. **"Of course! You remember that time when we were in London and you asked me to marry by putting a ring in my champagne?"** said Jill with an excitement. "A ring, yeah I remember", he said with a witty smile. "What?" she questioned. "You completely lost it", he mentioned. "No!" she said with a confidence in her voice. "Oh, you almost drank it", he explained. "So how would one know if there's a ring in the glass", she asked. "Anyone with a brain", he said while picking the napkin. "So anybody with a brain has made a burger for her own. Sir, you can stand and try your hands in the kitchen", she said with anger in her voice. "Oh, I was kidding. You took my words on your heart", he said after surrendering in front of Jill. "No, you will make things on your own. I am ready with my own burger and fries", she said while adding salt, garlic powder and pepper in her fries.

Matt instantly stood up and hugged Jill from behind. "I am sorry. I didn't mean to hurt you. It was purely sarcastic and said absolutely out of fun", he explained. "Don't you think I have a brain?" she asked while turning her face towards him. "No, I believe you are the smartest one in the room", he said. "You are saying this because you don't know how to make burgers, right?" she asked with a frowning face. "No, I am not saying this for any personal means. I am sorry", he said lowering his head slightly. "So you won't repeat this the next time?" she asked with an exaggerated expression. "I will never make fun of you", he said while kissing her on the left cheek.

"Now, tell me. What would you like to have today?" asked Matt. "My plate is ready. Now, you tell me, what you are going to have?" asked Jill while showing him the prepared food items. "We have your favourite burger and potato fries", she added. "You look happy", he said while looking at Jill. **"I've poured my heart and soul into preparing this dinner for you" as she plated the dish.** He smiled and replied "Please make my fries a little spicy and add double patty in my burger".

Jill kept the plates on the table and extras in the middle while sitting near the Matt's chair. "Oh, I forgot to bring tomato ketchup", she said. "Let me get that", he said while moving out of the chair. "Here it is. Now, let's dig in", he added. "Where are the candles?" she asked. He looked at her while taking a bite of his burger, "I don't know". His speech muffled. "We were expected to have lights around us", she explained with a furrowed brow. Matt's fingers were dipped in the sauce, half burger inside his mouth and the other half in his plate. With his mouth wide open. It was visible that the man of the house was enjoying his dinner and was literally having fun while seeing his wife happy. She smiled and took a first bite from her burger. "Oh, yum", she exclaimed. He waited for a second and then moved his lips near hers. "Absolutely, yum!" he responded. She began to blush uncontrollably.

Both of them finished their plates and Matt stood up to wash his hands and mouth. Tomato ketchup stained his face. "This child!" Jill remarked. He went to the basin and washed a bit of himself by using mild soap and water to wash the area where it was a noticeable stain. He then rinsed it thoroughly, used the hand towel to dry his hands. "I am full and happy", he said. "The way to a man's heart is through his stomach seems to have come true", she said while cleaning the plates. "You know when I was four or maybe near to five, I dreamt of having a small family and a peaceful home", he explained while sitting on the slab. She gave the wet plates & towel to him while saying "You have worked so hard to be here" to which he replied "It is because of you." She smiled and replied "I don't remember much of my childhood but one thing was sure, I never thought of getting married". Giving the bowl to him, she added "But when I saw you, things fell into places and life seemed complete. You know everything was okay and marriage became actually easy with you." He kept everything aside, stood on his feet and held her by saying "I love you!"

After helping her in completing the basic chores, he went to hit the hay. She turned off the lights, checked the doors and went in the balcony. "I totally forgot to take the clothes inside", she said to herself while pulling the clothes drying rack. "Oh god, they are stiff and frozen. How did I forget this?" she kept feeling frustrated. "Okay, cool down. Not a big deal. Keep the rack in the hall, clothes will dry till the morning and everything will be fine", she assured herself after blowing out the air from her mouth and her hands folded. She later closed the balcony door and pressed the button on the side of the handle to lock it. Pulling the gate to check if it was locked, she spread the curtains evenly on the side window to cover it and pushed the rack to the hall. "Light is good & furnace is warm. Happy winters!" she said while gently touching the forearms to her shoulders.

She washed her face & feet, brushed her teeth, applied the moisturizer and took her eye mask from the panel. "Goodnight love", she said while Matt was having his tabloid in his hands and he seemed really busy. She snapped her fingers from a distance to get his attention "Sir, I said Goodnight". He looked at her and replied "Goodnight, beauty. I am tired too and will sleep in 5".

Jill wore her eye mask and pulled her blanket close to her chin. **The sheets were so cold, she couldn't help but shudder.** Matt smiled and moved his hand around her cheeks "Too cold, huh!" to which she replied "Quite". He moved near her and said "Come!" She shifted her back towards him. "Why aren't you wearing your socks?" he said while his legs touched hers. "I don't like them", she replied. **"But baby, it's freezing in here, and your feet are ice cold"**, he said. "Ish. They will be okay in sometime", she replied while squeezing her blanket cover.

Matt turned off the room lights and adjusted his space next to Jill. "I feel happy seeing you happy", he said while kissing her cheeks. Jill's eye mask was removed briefly. He adjusted it and laid down on bed. It was 01:01 AM. Her sleep was interrupted and she abruptly removed her mask. There was no light in the room. After checking the time, she turned her face towards her husband who was sleeping soundlessly. She touched his nose using her pinky finger and closed her eyes. After almost trying to sleep for next hour, she opened her eyes again and turned her back towards him to face the wall. Her eyes were wide open and all her body was settled under the blanket. There was nothing visible in the room. Suddenly her blanket started feeling heavy. It felt like someone was sitting on her. She turned to check if it was his leg but to her surprise, he was side sleeping in a log position. Peeping inside her blanket, she tried to understand the feeling but couldn't. Feeling confused, she thought of waking him but stopped herself from doing so. "What if there's nothing just a bad feeling", she murmured. While staying still for few minutes, she closed her eyes.

Jill woke up at 05:04 AM and checked the time, stretched and got out of bed to help her body fully transition from sleep. Holding a jar of water in her one hand and glass in another, she filled it and started drinking. Morning prayers while sitting on the bed were a part of daily rituals. She looked at Matt and breathed a few words in his ears. "Wake up!" she said softly. "Five more minutes" said Matt while showing his palm. "Okay! Only five" she replied and wore her slippers to enter the washroom.

Opening the tap, she washed herself up and took a shower.

After she took her what they say 'Me-Time', she stepped out. "Matt, you'll be late!" Jill warned. She shook his shoulder and warned "Matt, it's time now". He rubbed his eyes while half opening them, "What's the time?" to which she replied "05:58 AM". "Two more minutes then, wake me at 6", he said.

Jill went outside, turned on the stair lights to check on Laxie and Macy. She entered inside Macy's room and called her name, "Darling, wake up! We have to go to school today" and started caressing her hand. Macy was so deep in her sleep that after being wobbled too many times, she started feeling groggy. "Macy, honey! Okay take five more minutes but then do make sure you stand on your feet and walk straight inside the washroom", said Jill. "I am going to your sister's room", she added. Closing the door, she went to wake Laxie. "Honey, Good morning", said Jill while removing the curtains of her room. "Laxie, come on. We are getting late now. See, it's snowing so beautifully outside and you will absolutely miss it by being lazy-pazy", she added. Laxie replied with "hmm" by showing her agreement and pulled her blanket to cover her face. "Laxie, wake up darling", said Jill while taking an exit from her room.

"Laxie and Macy's school will begin at 10:00 AM today but they both take so much time in getting ready, god", said Jill to herself while switching off the staircase lights. Moving inside the hall, she checked the clothes and removed them from the rack, later placing them on the sofa. "I will arrange them later", she said. "Good morning", Matt said. "Do we have a newspaper?" he asked. "Let me check", she opened the main door and picked the newspaper which was seen lying on the floor and gave it to Matt. "I am going to read it before entering the washroom" he said. While tying her hair, she asked "Okay, so what will you have in your breakfast today?" He opened the newspaper and replied, "What do we have?" She scraped her scalp and said "Eggs, Bread, Butter, Fruits, Biscuits, Cereals and Pancakes. "Um, Scrambled Eggs for me", he replied after thinking for few seconds. "Oh and don't forget to add few veggies in it", he added. "Veggies?" she said while making a grumpy face. "Yeah, customization you know!" he said while sitting on one side of the sofa and looking at the newspaper.

Jill picked four eggs from the carton and placed on the slab. Taking out the bowl, she crackled the eggs one by one in it. Using a fork, she beat the eggs until yolks and whites were fully combined. After this, she added a pinch of salt, pepper, few herbs and cheese. Placing a non-stick skillet pan over medium-low heat, she started to melt the butter in it and poured the beaten eggs into the pan. While they were cooking, she chopped few vegetables on the board and put them aside for a while. Using a spatula, she stirred and pushed the eggs for some time and then transferred the scrambled eggs to a plate. Topped those raw veggies on the prepared dish and kept the plate on the dining table. "Breakfast is ready, Matt. I am hoping to see you here as soon as possible", she announced and went back to pour some orange juice in a glass and later kept it near the plate. After untwisting the seal of bread, she picked two slices and kept them in a different plate. Using a butter knife, she took a scoop out a small amount of butter from the jar and spread the butter outward to cover the buttered slice of bread with the plain one and kept it on the plate. "Matt, eggs are turning cold now", she said in an audible tone.

Simultaneously, Matt was wearing his white shirt paired with black trousers. He then wore the thermal and the puffer jacket to resist cold. "Coming, J", he answered. Took the comb to set his hair, drank some water from the glass and left the room. "You always get late and then take your breakfast in haste", she said. "With this, I forgot to give you the soaked nuts. You can start with the eggs, I'll bring the nuts", she added and went to the kitchen. After taking out the bowl of nuts into a colander, she gently shook it to let the excess water to drain out and used the paper towel to pat the nuts dry. "Take these", she said. "You make the most amazing scrambled eggs but not as good as I do", he said with flying kiss. "You never miss a chance to make me blush", she said while smiling. He held the bread and took a bite from it. "Yum!" he teased. She looked at him with a wide smile and replied "Need milk? I have served the juice because you told me earlier". He took a sip and winked, "I am okay with it. It is yum too!" While standing up, he wiped his lips with the napkin, washed his hands and quickly grabbed his bag. "I am leaving. I will be back on time", he said while giving a side hug to her. She hugged him tightly and gave a peck on his lips. "Stay this cool, forever". He smiled and took his car keys, meanwhile she stood near the main door to watch him leave safely. "Bye!" she waved her right hand and shut the door. Stood near the dining table, kept the glass on the plate and went to keep it in a sink. "I need to chop some vegetables. Um, it's better I try something with the capsicum", saying this, she opened the fridge to take a bag of capsicums and placed them on the kitchen slab, near the stove.

Her phone chimed. She unlocked it to check the message which was from Jacob. "I expect you to complete the article by EOD", it read. "Sure!" she said to herself before typing. It was raining outside, she typed, "Sir, if it is fine then can I work from home today?" and kept staring at the screen until a text flashed, "As you like, but EOD means it's urgent". She nodded her head in acceptance, locked her phone and kept it on microwave oven. "Such a relaxing day", she said to herself while taking a sip of her coffee.

While she was managing the basic routine, her mind suddenly shifted towards Macy and Laxie. "The girls", she tapped the back of her head and climbed the stairs to enter into the Macy's room. "Macy! Macy!" She removed the blanket from the bed but she was not on bed. "Macy, Macy" she repeatedly called her name and knocked the bathroom's door but it was open. "Where is Macy?" she said to herself with panic covering all her face and immediately ran into Laxie's room taking their names. "Girls! Mommy is serious now, where are you?" she said. "I am closing my eyes and will count till three. Just come out, 3, 2, 1" she added and later opened her eyes but there was no sign.

Jill kept her left hand on her waist and held the forehead using her right hand. Darkness covered her eyes and she was not able to understand what to do next and immediately ran downstairs to pick her mobile phone. "I should call Matt", she murmured and kept dialling his number but it was not reachable. "Backyard!" she said in an assured tone. "Maybe they are outside in the search of sticks like before" she said while running outside. Both the girls were not there and when unable to find them, she sat down on her knees.

It was freezing cold outside but it seemed as if the coldness was ineffective on Jill. Realizing the girls were nowhere visible, she stood and ran inside again. "I should check the store. Macy must be playing with her doll there", she thought and instantly ran towards the store room. "Macy! Caught you!" **She said as** she switched on the lights, but her expression changed and she felt disappointed. "Where are my girls?" she said while sitting near the sofa and started sobbing. "Macy! Laxie!" said Jill in a soft voice and suddenly her head touched the floor. She fainted as tears continued to fall down her cheeks. After lying on the floor for almost an hour, she partially regained her consciousness and used her left hand to provide a support to her head. Cradling her head in her hands, she recalled what had happened around her before she collapsed on the floor. "My girls! My girls!" she screamed powerlessly.

Feeling dizzy, she stood up using the support of nearby objects. Her legs were trembling and it was very hard for her to even take a smallest step. With a severe pain in her head, confusion started to cover her eyes. "What is happening?" she said while tears started settling around the corner of her eyes. There was silence all over the place. Only the rain droplets were making their way outside the window panel. Suddenly, there was a knock on the door. With time, the sound started to increase and was audible in a better way. With the effect of excessive sound, she opened her eyes. It was unbearable for her to even let the light enter her vision. She rubbed her eyes while questioning about her present situation, "How did I come here?" Gathering all her strength to stand and walk, she answered "Coming" in a very hushed tone.

The moment door opened, she was in shock. The girls were standing in front of her eyes which made her drop to her knees with tears falling down. "Where were you? Where?" her voice broke. Macy and Laxie looked at each other and then used their hands to wipe Jill's tears. "Don't cry, Mommy". Jill made an eye contact with Laxie and asked, "Where were you?" to which Macy replied "School". Laxie looked at Macy and then shifted her eyes towards Jill to reply "Yes, Mommy. You dropped us to school in the morning". Jill wasn't able to recall what the girls were explaining. "I dropped you to school?" she asked. "Yes!" Macy replied. "You combed our hair, made us wear the uniforms, prepared our tiffins and handed the school bags to us. You even told us to bring the flowers for you from the school" she added. Hearing this, Jill felt puzzled. She fell out of words and was finding hard to understand how exactly to respond. "Are you sure?" she asked. "Yes, Mommy" replied Laxie and hugged her mother. "And tell us, why were you crying?" she questioned. On hearing this, Jill's eyes welled up again and she replied "Because I couldn't find you both". Laxie and Macy held Jill's hand and one of them questioned "How will you find us when we were not home?" Both of them kept their hands wrapped around Jill until she felt better.

Jill locked the door and questioned, "One second, how did you manage to come back home if I didn't go to pick you up?" Macy turned her face and replied "Our mentor was kind enough to drop us back home". "Who Mentor?" asked Jill. "You don't know her mom, she is nice", said Laxie and kept her school bag on the couch. It was just like a dream for Jill. She was not able to reciprocate properly to whatever was happening around her in that moment. Before she could speak again, her doorbell rang. "Now, who is it?" she turned to open the door. "Yes?" she asked to the man who was standing in front of her, a post boy. He touched his cap and replied "Ma'am, does Matt Charles live here?". She took a glance at him and asked, "I am his wife. Tell me?" He was shivering while they were talking. The boy looked in Jill's eyes and replied "Ma'am, here is the envelope". He gave it to her, took an acceptance signature on the paper and turned to walk out but Jill stopped him to enquire "Why are you not completely covered? I mean it is too cold". The boy turned around and replied in a humble tone, "Because of rain, my jacket became wet and I couldn't wear it Ma'am". Jill took a second before responding "Do you want to stop by?" The boy disagreed and thanked Jill for showing the concern. After handing the letter to her, he stepped down the stairs and left. Jill smiled and shut the door back. "Strange boy! Feeling cold but disinterested in taking the help", she said to herself. "Maybe he has his own reasons", she said in his defense.   She then opened the envelope which was addressed on Matt's name and it was from his office's headquarters, which read

"Dear Matt Charles,

*Congratulations on your promotion in Exilir! We are delighted to offer you the position of **Marketing coordinator** with an anticipated start date of 12th January'12.*

As discussed, you are immensely outstanding at the work so, accept this offer and confirm your answer. In addition to this, please sign, scan, and email your letter to us at elixir_ab@xwsyz.comm

In the meantime, please don't hesitate to reach out to us, either through email or by calling us directly at 60X0980.

We are looking forward to hear from you and hope you'll join our team!

Best regards,

Ben Clintonn

Chief Executive officer"

After reading this letter, she was really happy and instantly texted Matt regarding the same. "Oh my god! This is such a great news", she said to herself while her hands covering the mouth because of surprise. "This man is always late on his breakfast but promotions, ahhan cute", she added.

In this entire hustle, Jill completely forgot about the last incident. Macy and Laxie were seen playing in as they came from school. "Who is going to change the uniforms?" asked Jill. Laxie jumped out of the sofa and giggled, "You!" After reading the news, Jill's mood became joyful. She kept the letter on the dining table and put the paper weight on it.

"What? *smile emoji inserted", a text came from Matt. Jill smiled and replied back "What, What? You didn't know?" she asked. Before Jill could hit on send, Matt's text came "I wanted to surprise you but…" She backspaced the text and replied "Party!! *fun emoji inserted".

Keeping her phone aside, she felt a strong urge to eat something because she hadn't had anything since morning. "Macy, Laxie. What to make for you?" Jill asked. Macy came running and answered "Mommy, we had our lunch very late due to shift in PT period. So, can I skip for now? Laxie will tell her 'gut feeling'". Hearing which, Jill smiled and questioned "From where are you learning such phrases, huh?" to which Macy answered "Straight from my gut". "Okay, call Laxie", Jill ordered. Macy sent Laxie to her mother. "Lax, what would you like to have in lunch?" she asked. Laxie too had her lunch so she denied on the same and asked for some time later. "Okay, go and change your uniforms before you get indulged into something unusual", said Jill. Laxie showed a 'V-Sign' and ran away.

Jill started slicing vegetables, "I can make vegetable noodles for myself". She took out the different bell peppers, onions, potatoes, green cabbage, beans, garlic, mushrooms and ginger. "Maybe I can avoid putting ginger, the taste is quite extreme", she said. While chopping the vegetables into bit-sized pieces, her mind diverted towards missing Laxie and Macy incident. "How could I forget dropping them to school and who is this mentor? How had I not met her?" she said in a very suspicious tone. "I never forgot things in life but what is happening these days?" she continued. Her hands were continuously working on the board and mind was wandering all over the place. "I think I should inform Matt and I called him but his phone was not reachable", she said while wiping her hands over the apron. She took the phone in her hands and opened call logs. To her surprise, there was no call made to Matt. "How is this possible, now?" she said while staring at the curtain hanged near the wall. "I think my phone has turned into a scrap", she assured herself.

After giving a lot pressure on her memory, she dismissed everything by saying "Okay, let it be Jill. Maybe you forgot, that's normal for normal people". She kept the phone near the Matt's promotion letter and went inside to prepare her food. "I haven't written a word and deadline itself is today. I should hurry now", she said and opened the side drawer of the slab, later grabbed the packet of noodles. She flipped the packet to check if there were any instructions written and then kept a large skillet over a medium heat. Added minced garlic and stirred for about thirty seconds until fragrance covered the hall. She added the sliced mushrooms to the pan and cooked until they turned slight brown and released their moisture, for nearly five minutes. Adding other vegetables, she kept stirring for additional three to five minutes, until they got crispy. On the other stove, she boiled the noodles and then added them in the skillet. She poured some soy sauce, tossed everything together to make sure the noodles and vegetables were well-coated with the sauces. She drizzled some sesame oil and gave it a final toss. "Ah, it smells nice", she said in a very proud tone. She then took a fork to taste some and adjusted some seasoning with salt and pepper. "Not bad Jill", she said to herself. "You're quite improving", she continued.

After taking out the noodles on plate, she kept her 'used fork' in it. "Shall I put some green onions", she placed her finger under her chin to clear her confusion. "Leave it, I can have it as it is". She kept the used skillet in the sink and said "From the time Jimmy had stopped coming, it has become easy to experiment things in the kitchen. Otherwise, she never let me enter inside it". After taking the bowl in her left hand, she went inside to sit on the sofa and kept the bowl on the table. She started searching for the television remote. "It has been ages, I haven't watched anything on it" she said while jerking her neck.

"I should have added some soup in it", she said to herself while changing the channels. She twirled the small portion of noodles around the tines of fork. "There's nothing good to watch. By the time I will find something, my bowl will be empty", she said while making a classic sad face and turned off the television. "Delectable", she said. "To eat in such an amazing weather is a blessing", she continued speaking with a smile on her face. "Macy, Laxie, are you sure you don't want the last bite?" Jill announced. "No, Mommy. We are full", she said while throwing the fur in the air. "Where did you find this cotton fur?" Jill questioned while chewing her noodles. "From the pillow", Laxie replied. "Girls!" Jill emphasized. "I told you to not create a ruckus", she kept saying. "Mommy, we will not disturb the setup. We are playing silently", Macy replied politely. Jill slowly closed her eyes, stating her agreement. Jill again picked the fork to continue eating.

While she was taking a bite from her bowl, she observed that the sofa had an impression of someone sitting beside her, almost close to her. She touched the fabric with her trembling hands and kept touching it for about 2-3 times. She removed her hand and felt doubtful. The sofa again got back to normal. "Maybe I sat there in the first place and then shifted on the other side. After observing for a while, there was no change so she again shifted her eyes towards the bowl. "My stomach is at capacity and I still have to take two more bites", Jill said while keeping her empty hand on her stomach and leaning back. She shifted her eyes on the side of her sofa but there was no change. "Hilarious!" she said and the stood up to keep the bowl in the kitchen.

"Girls, need milk", Jill asked. "One for me!" Macy announced. "Laxie, what will you take?" Jill asked. "Only water", Laxie replied. "Oh! Come here and take it", Jill said while keeping both her hands around her waist. She poured the milk in the glass and left it on slab. "Time to open the laptop", she said while looking at the time on the clock. She went inside her room to get the laptop, touched the power button and entered the password once the laptop finished booting. She opened her office's portal and checked the status of the recent articles posted by her company and then opened her document to begin writing. "Um, I should sit outside but it's raining and too cold. I shall sit on the study table", she said and took her laptop to sit on the study table.

"Self-love makes you feel alive. Have you ever sat along in a balcony, sipping the coffee, feeling the air on your cheeks? Even the thought gives me smile so think about that feeling. I must not restrict this 'self-love' within some brackets because it is free, it flies free in the air and spreads from door to door. Life feels amazing when you realize your own importance, value your emotions, respect your boundaries, create room and space for your own thoughts instead of world throwing the tags on you." Jill kept writing and this time, all the thoughts were flowing out of her mind. She felt happy after completing four and half pages. "I think I have written enough", she said to herself while reading the article again from the top.

Jill took approximately three hours to put her thoughts on the paper and later grabbed her phone to call Jacob. There was no answer from his side so she dropped a voicemail, "Boss, I have completed the article and mailing you in a while. Please go through it and suggest the changes, if there are any". She then attached the document in mail and sent it to him. It was quarter past six on the clock, she put the laptop on sleep mode and left it on the study table.

"So much snow!" she said while peeping out of the window. "This is really strange that Jimmy neither came nor replied to phone call. Is she okay?" she continued. "Should I call her again?" she questioned. "I think I should. It is my responsibility to check on her", she said while searching for her phone. "Caught you!" she said while taking her phone in her hands. "Um.. Jimmy.. Jimmy..", she kept saying while scrolling her name in the contact list. She tapped on the 'Phone' icon in order to give a call to her, yet again there was no answer. "What has happened?" she said. Her phone started to ring, it was from Jacob. "Boss?" she remarked. She swiped the ringing icon and answered "Hello?" Jacob greeted her and said "I received your mail. The article is fine but can we add more points. I mean 'Self-love' is a vast topic". Jill heard him carefully and replied "Yes, Sir. I'll look into it". Jacob took a moment and replied "You can submit it till tomorrow noon. But not beyond that". Jill replied while touching the right side of her neck with her left hand, "Sure, Sir. Thank you for extending the deadline". She disconnected the call and kept the phone near the laptop.

"Today was such a busy day. There's no sign of Jimmy and I need to clean the entire home now", she said while entering the store room. She took out the vacuum cleaner and kept it against the wall. Then picked the large items and arranged them in an unoccupied area. She went to check the vacuum bag if it was empty. "Let's start from my room", she said while holding the stick of cleaner and began vacuuming in one corner of the room, making her way towards the exit. Later entering into the hall, cleaned it, following the kitchen and store room. She then went upstairs and barged in Macy's room. After moving the cleaner in all the corners of the room, she took an exit.

"Laxie, Macy, where are you?" she questioned. Laxie was sitting at her room's gate. "What are you doing here? You could have got hurt", Jill said with concern in her voice. "We are playing", she replied. "Where's Macy?" Jill questioned. "Under the bed", Laxie replied while pointing towards the legs of her bed. "What game is it? Come on now, get up. I have to clean the room", Jill said. Macy and Laxie ran downstairs and started playing in the hall. "Do not sit on the floor. It's really cold", Jill shouted from the Laxie's room.

"Mom, can we add some sticks in the furnace?" Macy questioned. "Not until I come downstairs", replied Jill with all the background noise. She cleaned the room, checked the stairs, came downstairs and put the vacuum in the balcony. "You should not go near to the fire if I am not there near to you", Jill instructed. "Got me?" she asked. Macy nodded her head in the agreement. "Come we will add sticks together. Let me wash my hands first", Jill said and went near the basin. "Laxie, Mommy is allowing us to put sticks in the furnace. Come!" said Macy with an excitement in her tone. Laxie came running towards Jill and Macy. All three of them went near the furnace. Jill opened the bag and picked some sticks from it. "Okay, so before you put them into fire, check if they are properly seasoned and dry otherwise there will be smoke in the hall or they might not burn efficiently", Jill guided. "Then open the door of the wood burning furnace and place the sticks inside it. First add smaller sticks and then the larger ones. Make sure you check the proper airflow so that they could burn in an effective manner. Once all the sticks are arranged, close the door very carefully. Be aware to not burn your hand in the process. Always check for the air flow. Our home will stay warm this way", she continued. "This is beyond amazing", said Laxie. "I agree", said Macy. "Can we try putting one or two sticks?" questioned Laxie. "Sure", said Jill while reopening the furnace door. "Now, pick one stick, slightly bend and put the stick inside it attentively", Jill commanded.

Laxie and Macy picked sticks one after the other and put them inside the furnace. "This was easy", said Laxie. "It is but stay cautious", said Jill and stood up. "Now, close the door and maintain some distance from it", she continued. Both the girls closed the door and went to play. "Just a moment – have you both completed your homework?" Jill asked. "Um, we haven't", replied Macy with a guilt in her voice. "Then when will you start doing it? It's already 19:35 PM", questioned Jill. "We have not done because teacher didn't give any today", replied Laxie and both of them started laughing. "Are you fooling me?" asked Jill in a humorous way. Jill felt relaxed seeing the girls happy. She never imagined her life without them.

"With this I forgot that we have no vegetables left. And I definitely cannot expect vegetable truck to come", she said to herself. "Macy, Laxie, would you mind If I got out and grab some vegetables real quick?" Jill questioned. Macy looked at Laxie before replying. "Can we go with you, please?" Macy requested. "Baby, I will take ten minutes only. See, I have to buy some vegetables before it starts snowing again. We have red alerts in our area", Jill responded. "Mommy, please bring us the candies", said Laxie. "Girls it is not nice to act like this. I will come back quickly", Jill said in a rigid tone. "Okay!" replied Laxie with a sad face. "Let's play Macy", she continued.

Jill's heart started feeling heavy so she took a pause and said "Okay, we are going. But wear your jackets properly. It is really cold outside". Jill took her jacket and wore it. "I need a cap too", she said to herself and went inside her bedroom. "Okay. Are we ready?" asked Jill. "Yes, Mommy", replied Macy. "And we will buy some candies", she added. Jill looked at Macy and said "We are not going to stop anywhere except the vegetable market. I wouldn't have taken the risk if there hadn't been any alert news".

"Where is your jacket, child?" questioned Jill while looking towards Laxie. "I am wearing the thermal inner and Mommy we will stay back in the car, so I won't feel anything extreme", Laxie replied. "No. You're wearing the jacket right away otherwise no one is going", Jill ordered. Laxie thumped her feet and went upstairs to wear the cover herself. "Macy, sweetie, it is very important for you to understand about the dangers. It is really cold outside, you have experienced it yesterday. Believe me, I pray and want you to stay fit by avoiding such risks", Jill explained her fear to Macy. Meanwhile Laxie came downstairs wearing one sweater and an overcoat. "That's like my girl", Jill said while running her fingers through Laxie's hair.

"Come on, Now. Get inside the car", Jill said while taking the car keys, home keys, purse and the phone. She locked the door once everyone stepped out and then unlocked the car gates. Macy and Laxie sat at the backseat. Jill sat on the driver's seat and questioned "No one on my passenger seat today?" Macy looked at Laxie and went outside the car. She opened the gate of the car's front side and sat next to Jill. "Put your seatbelts", said Jill. Laxie and Macy pulled their seatbelts and locked them. "Let's go!" Macy exclaimed.

"Mommy, why does it snow?" Laxie questioned. "It snows due to cold temperatures in our areas. It depends on many factors including moisture, geography and climate that helps in snow formation", said Jill while reducing the speed of her car and taking the turn. Macy was looking outside her window and while watching so much snow on the road she questioned "Mommy, do you ever feel scared while driving around the snow?" This was a different question for Jill. Fear is something that is an emotional response to a perceived threat. Jill exhaled her breath and replied "We do feel scared sometimes. And, yes I turn attentive when you both are with me in such situations especially heavy snow and rains".

"Mommy, how come you remember all the lanes. You don't even use maps" asked Laxie. "Because when you do the same thing several times, like walking on these lanes again and again, your memory captures and stores the images which later help you to reconnect", replied Jill with all the patience she had in her. After several turns, they reached to the vegetable market.

"Okay, now listen to me. I am keeping your side windows slightly open and locking the car from outside. Stay inside till I come and if you feel anything wrong, then call my name", Jill instructed while pressing the button of her seatbelt. "Promise me, you'll stay safe inside. And do not fight and create a problem for me", she added. "We promise, Mommy!" both said in unison. Jill gave an assured smile and stepped out of the car. "She locked the gate, looked at the girls and went to buy vegetables". She had a list in her hand and since it was snowing, there were very few people in the market. "I think I am late", she said to herself.

The market was U-Shaped, so she started from her left side. "I will take the vegetables that are firm, vibrant in color and free from blemishes", she thought. After spending twenty minutes in the market, her basket was full with the variety. She then went on the counter and kept the basket on the desk for the billing. She stood near the heater and waited for the man to acknowledge her presence. While standing there, she kept an eye on her car and once their eyes met, she smiled at the girls. "Coming, two minutes", her lips moved.

The man sitting on the desk checked the vegetables, weighed them and gave the bill to Jill. After exchanging the bag with money, she started walking towards her car. Even after walking far away from the heater, there was so much warmth in her left hand. She took the bag in her right hand and checked her palm. "I am not even wearing gloves in this hand but I still feel heat in it", she said to herself. Her right hand was completely normal. She was baffled. She took all the items in her right hand and set the left hand free. "It will get normal in sometime", she said to herself. She unlocked the car, kept the bags near Laxie at the backseat, opened the front gate and sat inside, handing over her phone and bag to Macy.

"Mommy, you were so quick", said Macy. "Yes, because you two were alone in the car", she said while looking at Macy and then at Laxie. "Okay, time for candies now", she continued. Macy and Laxie looked at each other with the excitement. "We are so happy", said Macy. "What do you want to have in dinner?" asked Jill. "Not at home. We want to go to 'Frankie love'" said Laxie while bouncing up and down on her seat. "Frankies?" asked Jill. "At this time?" she continued. "Mommy we have burgers at this time. Frankies are lighter than them", replied Laxie. "Girls we have been eating junk from a few days now. Let's cut it today", said Jill while adjusting the shoulder strap. "But Mommy, New Year vibes", replied Macy. "Two days left" said Macy while moving her head in agreement, "Still", Jill paused. "Mommy please", Laxie requested. "Okay, but no junks after today", said Jill. "By the way, Mommy. We have holidays from tomorrow. Schools will reopen on 8th January", said Macy. "And you're telling me now?" asked Jill while moving the steering. Macy smiled and replied "We forgot to tell you", said Macy while touching her scalp. Jill smirked and said "Okay. Put the destination in maps. I think I am missing the right lane".

Laxie took the phone from Macy's hand, showed the screen to Jill to unlock it and then opened Maps. "Mommy, you need to take the second left turn, drive 1 km straight and then take second right from the circle", Laxie guided. "Not bad. You have not only started reading maps but also giving instructions", said Jill with a surprise in her expression. All three of them reached the 'Frankie love', both the girls stepped out and stood near the pole. Jill lowered the window and said "Baby, Stay there. I am parking the car". After applying the reverse gear, she parked her car and stepped out.

Jill made the girls sit on the chair and told them to wait. She then went to the counter to ask for the menu which was already displayed on the boards above the counter. "Hello, Ma'am. Welcome to the Frankie love. How can I help you?" the woman standing on the counter said. Jill smiled and replied, "Hi, Actually I want the menu". The woman said "Ma'am, the list is already visible on the top and here, take this". The woman handed over the glossy paper to Jill which she took and went to the girls. "See this", Jill said while giving it to them. "Yayayayae!" replied Macy. "Well, I have this specific type on my mind. Can I order it mum?" said Laxie. "Yes!" Jill said with hesitation in her voice. "I will take Egg frankie with Mexican touch", said Laxie. "Nice, from where are you learning these terms?" asked Jill. With a surprise in her tone. "Um, and I will have Mixed Vegetable Frankie" said Macy. "Okay, Noted Ma'am" Jill replied and took the menu from her hands. "Laxie, sweetie I need to confirm if they have this combination available", said Jill. She then went to the woman on the counter and enquired "Ma'am, Please take my order. One Vegetable frankie, One mushroom frankie and um..", she took a pause before continuing "Do you have Egg Frankie with Mexican touch?" The woman entered the vegetable and mushroom Frankies in her computer. The woman then discussed it one of the chefs and responded politely "Yes, Ma'am. It is available". Jill beamed and replied "Okay, please make it one. And oh, do you have juices?" The woman replied "Yes, Ma'am. We have Orange, Berry, Grape, Pineapple, Tomato, Pomegranate, Apple, Cranberry and Mango juice. What can I add for you, Ma'am?" Jill took a while and then replied "One second, Ma'am". She went to the girls. "Do you feel like taking the juice, a healthy one", said Jill. "Orange", said Macy. "Pomegranate", said Laxie while her one hand up In the air. "Okay", Jill smiled and went back to the woman to finalize the order. "Ma'am, make one glass each of Pomegranate and Orange juices. And also, make Tomato soup for me. I saw it in the menu", said Jill. The woman entered the data in the computer and told the final amount to Jill. She exchanged the money with the receipt and thanked the woman.

All three of them patiently waited for their receipt number to show on the board were seen discussing about the 'New Year'.

Jill's phone started to ring, it was from Ayra. She answered the phone and said "Hello?" to which Ayra replied "Ya, Hi Jill!" She took a pause and then continued, "Are you home or in office?" Jill chortled and said "Nope. Not at work but came to buy vegetables" Ayra replied, "Oh, Okay. Actually I called you to invite you for our New Year party. We are hosting it at our place". Jill smiled and replied "That is so great" Ayra grinned "Actually we three wanted to give the invitation to you in person" Jill's eyes lit up when she heard 'we', "Three? Oh my god, are you expecting?" Ayra nodded her head before saying a 'Yes'. "Wow, I am so happy for you Ayra! Finally!" Jill responded with the gratefulness in her expressions. "Thank you so much. Well, I wanted to meet and tell you this. So, I hope to see you tomorrow", said Ayra with happiness in her voice. "Yes, definitely. In fact I am on my way back home, can meet you in next half an hour. Even Matt will be home by then", replied Jill while scratching her earlobe. "Okay, will inform you. For now, I and Liam are distributing the invitation cards among our friends since the occasion is very near", Ayra informed. "No worries. No worries", Jill blabbered. "You can join us anytime you like", she continued. "Okay!" replied Ayra and disconnected the call.

"Woof!" said Laxie while Jill almost dropping her phone on the floor. "You caught me off guard, darling. What are you doing?" asked Jill. "I was scaring you, Mommy", replied Laxie in a funny way. "That's not funny, baby. I could have dropped my phone", Jill replied while moving her fingers inside Laxie's hair. "Order No 365", counter person announced. Jill heard the number and looked at the bill. "It's ours", she said and stood up from her chair. She went to the counter and showed the bill, "It's my order". The woman smiled and handed over the tray to her saying "Take it, Ma'am".

Jill took the tray, went back to her seat "Frankies for you, darlings" Macy and Laxie apparently jumped on the tray to take their wraps. "It's mine", said Laxie while snatching the Macy's Frankie. "They have mentioned the types. Macy show me the wrap in your hand", asked Jill. Macy showed the wrapped paper to Jill with a saddened face expressions. "See, it's mine", Macy said in a very low voice. "My sweety, yes, Laxie it's hers", Jill replied while making a puppy face.

Laxie and Macy started eating their Frankies and Jill asked them to pose for a picture. "You're looking so cute", said Jill. All three of them had a small party. "Now, let's go", said Jill while picking her car keys and purse from the table. "Have you had enough? Do you wish to take anything else", asked Jill. "Mommy, can we buy candies as well?" asked Laxie. "From here?" questioned Jill. "If that is possible for you then yes", Macy winked towards Laxie. "From where are you guys learning all this, huh?" asked Jill with confusion in her eyes. "School teaches something, Mommy", replied Laxie while giving a high-five to Macy.

Jill held fingers of both the girls and took an exit from the place. "Get in the car", said Jill. She sat on the wheel and started the car. "So, where now?" asked Laxie. "Home!" replied Jill. "No, Mommy. Candies", said Macy. "Girls, you have started inculcating this in your habit, not listening to me and disrespecting", said Jill while being interrupted by Laxie "disrespecting?" Jill nodded her head and replied "Yes". Macy and Laxie stopped saying anything. Jill drove the car home and both the girls stepped out in anger. "We never disrespect", said Macy to Laxie. "We never did", Laxie responded back. Both the girls were waiting for their mother to park the car and open the main gate. Jill locked the car gate and opened the main door which Laxie and Macy pushed and went inside. Jill closed the door back and said "Girls, this is not the right behaviour. Come here and discuss with me". Girls climbed the stairs and went to their rooms. Jill held the baluster, stood near the last stair and shouted their names. "Macy, Laxie. Come downstairs". Silence covered the hall, making Jill feel more disappointed.

Jill sighed and went to her bedroom. She faced herself in the mirror and questioned "Am I not a good mother?" She stayed still for a while and her doorbell rang. "Why did they say such things for me?" she continued speaking and kept staring without blinking her eyes. The doorbell rang again, and this time thrice in a row. Jill instantly came out of her bubble of thoughts and ran towards the door. "Who is it?" she said and opened the door. To her surprise, there was no one near the entryway. "Ah, who is it?" Jill stepped out and started searching. "Who rang it?" she said to herself and went inside. The moment she closed the door, someone rang the bell again and this time continuously. She immediately peeped out of the window and then opened the door. "Who? I said who it is?" she shouted. "I am not going to go inside until you show up", said Jill while folding her hands around her chest. "Is this a joke? Stop pranking", she said after waiting for five minutes. She started taking brisk walk outside her doorstep to make sure she didn't miss out this time. After half an hour passed, Jill's frustration level reached the heights. "I am so angry right now. We should really put cameras outside our place", she went inside while talking to herself. She shut the door back and the bell started to ring again. She clenched her fists and decided not to open the door. "I am not going to open, keep pressing", she said and moved inside the kitchen. She poured the water in glass and took small sips out of it.

The bell was ringing continuously and later her phone started ringing. She checked her phone. The call was from Matt. "Matt?" she said and answered the call. "Hello?" said Jill. "Hello? Are you not home?" asked Matt. "I am", she replied. "Then why ain't you opening the door?" he asked. "Are you standing outside" questioned Jill while shifted the curtains slightly. Matt was standing there with both the hands open in air. "From past ten minutes", he replied. She immediately opened the door and said "I am sorry but.." Matt interrupted in between and said "But, babe? You knew I was ringing the bell?" Jill denied by shaking her head while drowning in tears. She used the back of her hand and wiped her tears. "Matt..believe me", she stammered. "Hey? Why are you crying? I didn't mean to hurt you" said Matt. "Okay, sit here. Tell me what it is?" he continued. "Someone..someone was ringing the bell..bell continuously and when I opened the door to check, nobody..nobody was there", she broke in tears. "Jill", he said while supporting her cheek with his palm. "It's okay! It's fine". Matt took out his handkerchief and gently dabbed at her eyes. "I think you've been punked!" he said in a tender voice. "It's okay", he held her chin with both his hands.
Matt loosened the tie knot and went in the kitchen to bring the glass of water. He took the glass placed on the slab and gave it to her. "Drink this!" he commanded. She took a sip and said "Freshen up! I will prepare the dinner for us". He gave an assured smile to her, locked the main door and went inside his room. She stayed at her place for some time and then went inside the kitchen. While she was taking out the bowl from the

drawer, he came out and said "Let's order it from outside. Don't take so much stress". She disagreed to the statement first but he convinced her.

Jill gave a forced smile and said "Okay!" Matt came close to her and said "Don't worry sweety. I am here for you, Always!" There was so much warmness in Matt's voice that made her weak to her knees. "You make me complete", she said. "Now, tell me. What would you like to eat?" he questioned. "Well, I am quite full right now. So I'll take some dessert to eat", she said with quirky smile. "Ah! What made you so full?" he asked while winking at her. "I ate rolls today, plus juice. Oh god! Too heavy", she replied. "Not bad! Okay, So um..I want to eat Spaghetti and Lasagna. What say?" he said with crinkling around the eyes. "Also, I won't mind your cheeks between my teeth" he continued. "Scary!" replied Jill while shifting her gaze. He grinned and looked at the clock. "We aren't that late. Give me that number..That outlet at the corner of our road", he said while furrowing his brows in concentration. "Alex's stop?" she questioned. "Yep, that's right. I have tasted Chinese noodles at his place and it was really amazing", he responded. She smiled and checked the number from the pocket diary "Okay! Dial 0921". She immediately thought of girls and shifted her eyes towards the stairs but then quickly shook her neck "They should realize their mistake". He immediately called, gave his order and sat on the sofa.

"It will take at least 30 minutes. I'm so hungry that I can hardly wait", he said. "Shall I quickly make something for you?" she asked. "No, No!" he said while wagging his index finger. "Come sit here", he continued while patting the seat. "I missed you!" she said. "Can we ever go back to our college days?" she asked with curiosity in her voice. "Practically, No! But Mentally,

Always!" he replied while crossing his legs on the centre table. "I miss our old times, sitting on the rooftop, feeling the air on our faces, eating ice creams even on the coldest nights, scrambling our names on the hostel walls. I mean good old days", she said while putting her head on his left shoulder. "And writing letters. What about them?" he said. "My heart is full", she said in a soft voice. "And my stomach is growling", he showed his soulful eyes.

"Twenty five minutes gone. The delivery boy must be on his way", she assured. "To walk just seven doors", he made a playful voice. In the middle of their discussion, doorbell rang, "My food!" he jumped out of sofa to open the door. "Such a kid!" she said while smiling. He took the parcel and paid the money. Happiness was visible all over his face. "You have been eating a lot junk lately", she teased. "We are young and not broke", he replied and kept the paper bag on the dining table.

"Let's dig in, baby!" he said to her. "I am brining the plates, hold your horses, Sir", she said and opened the drawer in the kitchen and took three plates, forks and bowls in her hands. "Give me, I will serve you", she continued. "No! No! Sit down with me", he said and held her hand. "Come-come", he immediately pulled out the chair and made her sit on it. "Okay, you are going to share with me. See, I have ordered for two", he said. "But I told you, I am full", she said while keeping her left hand on the stomach and wrinkles on her forehead. "Shh..", he said and opened the seal. He then transferred the spaghetti in the serving dishes and said "This is for you and me". "Steaming hot!" she said while appreciating the aroma. "Dessert for you! Oh, that's a surprise by the way", he said while raising his eyebrows and nodding his head. "Pecan pie", she said while unboxing. "Oh, I absolutely love it", she continued. "Pass me that plate, I need to transfer this cheesy cheese lasagna", he said.

Both of them ate their food. "That was a good heavy meal, wasn't it?" he mentioned. "Definitely! This lasagna has become one of my favourites and now I am so full. My stomach can burst", she replied. "Same! I need to take a walk", he said. "But such a brave heart. In this cold, they are delivering such good food", he continued. "Oh with this I remember, Ayra called to invite us on New Year. Ayra and Liam are hosting the event", she said. "New Year?" he questioned while wiping his face with the towel. "Yes, plus they are expecting", she replied while hiding her smile. "That's a news. This Lad!" he said with a relaxed face. "Shall I call him?" he asked. "At such Odd hour? Meet him tomorrow. They might come to give us an invitation card", she said while picking up the plates.

"I need to do some office work, you can take walk till then", she said and went inside the kitchen. She placed the dishes in the dishwasher. After completing her work, she took her laptop from the study table. "Shall I check upon the girls? They haven't come downstairs from a long time now", she said while looking at the time. "It's 12:04 AM. They must have slept", she said to herself. She left the laptop and went to Macy's room. She silently opened the door, both the girls were tucked inside their blankets. "Sleeping together today!" she said and closed the door. She made her way through the house with silent steps to avoid waking the girls and then took the phone, laptop in her hands. "Deadline's tomorrow, so need to work hard Jill", she bucked herself up.

"Matt, do you need anything because I'm working on my laptop now?" she asked. "Not much but could you refill this jar?" he said while giving the empty one to her. She filled the water in the jar and placed on his bedside table. "Anything else?" she asked. "You, maybe!" he replied while moving finger around the side of his forehead. She playfully touched him on his shoulders and replied "Ish! Get back to your reading now". She sat on the rocking chair in their room, cross folded her legs on the front table and placed the laptop on her lap. Both of them were doing their things silently, and after an hour, he dozed off. She looked at him and smiled, placed her laptop on the table and went to cover him using the blanket. She gave him a kiss on his head and went back to her seat.

Only the distinct clicking sound was heard in that room. It was past 1 AM on the clock. She rarely worked this late but since there were some strong instructions from the boss and major requirement in the organization, she had to take a toll. "I feel hungry now. I have eaten a lot in slots but still?" she said to herself and went straight in the kitchen to open the drawer. There were some packed chips available. She took the packet of soy sauce flavored rice chips. "I don't know how it tastes but ok..let me try" she murmured and closed the drawer.

While she was crossing the hall to enter her room, there was a drooping sound. She stopped at her place to concentrate on the source and then moved near the main door's window. The sound was now fading away. She stood there for a while and then the moment she started walking back, there was the sound again. A dripping sound this time. She was confused because it hadn't been audible earlier, so she went to check the faucet in the hall. "From where is it coming?" she grumbled and went near the window to check if it was raining. She peeped out of the window, there was snow all over the place but no sign of rain which made her feel stumped.

The dripping sound became more intense. She left the packet on the table and ran to check the tap of her bedroom's bathroom. She immediately opened the door, went near the basin and touched it. She then turned around and check the faucet, bath tub and shower. Going straight into her kitchen, she checked the dishwasher. "Is there any leakage but I don't think we have any other space where tap could be opened?" she questioned herself. "Kids room", she said and quickly climbed the stairs to check their bathrooms. To her surprise, there was no open or leaky tap in her home. She had to tiptoe quietly across the room to avoid waking the girls who were seen sleeping soundly in their bed. She shut the door back and whispered "I don't know.." All of a sudden, she realized that the sound was no more audible, it stopped. She came downstairs while her one hand sliding on the railing. While standing in the middle of the hall, she tried to analyze what happened around her. "I don't know from where that sound was coming", she muttered and picked the chips packet and went inside her room.

Jill sat on her chair and gently tore the packet using her canine. While opening, she held the packet firmly to minimize the crinkling sound and avoid waking Matt up. She placed the laptop on her lap and started eating while typing. "I have to complete it before the clock hits 2", she spoke softly. After minutes of running her fingers on the keyboard, she completed her article and mailed it to her Boss for the review. She then checked the messages on her phone and replied to some. "I am such an old school. Haven't checked my messages from ages", she whispered. Opening the chat box, she texted her boss, *"Sir, I have made some modifications and sent you the article on mail. Kindly review and suggest if there are any changes. Meanwhile, I will start working on the article titled as 'Women Empowerment' like we discussed in our monthly meeting"* and sent it. "I hope he doesn't reply to it", Jill said, thinking he might be online at that hour. She clicked on "Shut Down" to turn off the laptop and kept it on the Ottoman table. "Time to sleep now", she said while yawning.

After picking the packet from the table, she went to keep it back in the kitchen and gripped the handle firmly to pull the drawer straight out towards her. There was a constant thud sound coming from the corner of the hall. Since the lights were off, she was not able to see anything. "Matt?" she called his name. "Are you there?" she questioned and got really scared because even if it was Matt, he was not answering. "Matt?" she said and walked on the balls of her feet. "Matt, are you there?" her hands started shivering and voice trembled. The sound started growing louder. "Macy, Laxie? Are you...are you there?" her voice kept shaking. "See..this is not the right..right time to tease me like this", she continued. She went near the switch board and quickly turned on the flush mount lights. To her surprise, there was no one and the sound also stopped.

After spotting no one, her eyes opened wide indicating disbelief. Her mouth was slightly opened and forehead wrinkled due to raised eyebrows. She leaned her back gently against the wall for support. "I..I cannot believe..believe this", she stammered while speaking. She started taking deep breaths by inhaling slowly through her nose, held for few seconds and exhaled. She stood up and immediately ran towards her room

"Matt? Matt?" she started crying while calling out his name. Jill tapped lightly on his face and shook him. "Matt? Please wake up", she was unshakably crying. Matt suddenly opened his eyes and took a sitting position. "What..What happened, Jill?" he asked and immediately looked at the clock. It was 3:07 AM. He kept his hand on her cheeks and asked "Tell me, what happened?" He stayed composed while helping her respond effectively. "Ma..Matt..Someone was..was there outside", she said while pointing outside the door. "What?" Matt reacted surprisingly and stood out of bed to check. "But now there is no one", she answered while crying.

"Babe, look at me. Someone was there and now no one. What does that mean?" he expected an explanation. Jill took a deep breath and explained the narrative. "Believe me..Someone was there", she said. Matt held her hands and hugged her. He kept his palm on the back of her head and said "Sh! There is no one. You want me to go out and check?" Jill's chin touched his chest while she said "Someone was there". He took her hands in his hands and said "Come, we will check together". They went out and he switched on all the lights of the hall. "See, there's no one", he said. "Maybe the person..maybe the person hid behind something", she replied while moving the curtains. "Jill, there's no one. See, the doors are latched from inside and we are standing here from past five minutes. There's no sound and nobody is here", he assured. "You must be dreaming. See the time and you were working on the laptop from some time now, maybe you are seeing things but they are not real", he continued speaking while touching her shoulder. "Come, let's get inside", he said.

Both of them started walking toward the room but Jill kept her head turned and her eyes searching for the source of strange sounds. "Jill, no one is there. Come", he said while turning off the lights and made her sit on her side of bed. "Let's get cozy in bed and relax. It's a nice and comfortable place to unwind, okay", he extended his hand towards her face. "Don't turn off the lights please", she requested while lying flat on her bed. He ensured the pillow was positioned correctly to support her neck and head. "You are loved and cared for. Have a restful sleep, sweetheart", he said and shut the door. "Can we keep the lamps on?" Matt questioned while adjusting the blanket. Jill nodded her head. He turned off the big lights and sat on the bed. "Come here. Do you need your eye mask?" Matt questioned. "No, No", Jill's body language was conveying her fear and anxiety. "Do not worry. You have me", he replied and pulled her hand near him. Both of them laid on the bed while he kept patting her arm. "I love you", he said with a smile. She smiled back but did not utter a word. After some time, he slept while she was awake. Her eyes were wide open, it felt as if moisture had left her eyes.

Matt's hands were holding hers, she looked at the time. It was 4:09 AM, the ticking sound covered the room. She closed her eyes and had no idea when she fell into a deep sleep. Suddenly, a loud, jarring sound - a blaring alarm pierced through the silence. It was 5:00 AM and the buzzer made her wake abruptly. She pressed the button to stop the alarm. Because she was feeling super sleepy, she placed the pillow under her knees and slept on her back saying "Today is Macy and Laxie's day off. I can sleep for one hour more". She closed her eyes and later woke up at Matt's voice. It was 8:45 AM. He was sitting next to her, holding her hands. "Oh", she suddenly woke up which left her body tense and muscles rigid. She took the alarm clock and checked the timing. "Oh, I am so sorry Matt. I cou..", Jill started to speak and was interrupted by Matt in between. "It's okay. You slept late and don't worry about it. I am all ready, had bread and butter in the breakfast and drank juice from the fridge", he said. "I woke up at 5 but slept again. I am sorry", she explained. "It is perfectly okay. How do you feel now?" he asked. "Mortified", she replied while making a pout. "Why?" he questioned. "Because it never happened. I.." she spoke. "Some things happen for the first time and it is not the crime", he chuckled. "Now, I will be late in reporting, so you take your time. Just make sure to lock the door once I leave", he said while standing up.

"Shall I make something quickly?" asked Jill to make sure he had eaten fine. "I am full", he replied while rubbing his hand over his stomach dramatically. She stepped out of bed and tapped him on his back. "I feel so groggy. Waking up late makes human so lazy", she said while hugging him from the back. "Mrs. Charles, take a day off today. Solace!" he said while touching the back of her head using his left hand. "We were supposed to meet Liam and Ayra today. New Year's eve tomorrow", she said. "That is why, tomorrow is going to be company's day off but today we are closing the month targets. So, no baby! Have to go", he replied. She leaned her head around his neck and sighed "Okay! Me-time then".

Matt waved his hand and sat in his car while Jill stood near the doorstep. He smiled and reversed the car. After a few seconds, his car left the space. She shut the door and went inside her room to freshen up. "9 AM", she said while looking at the clock. Before entering the bathroom, she picked her phone to check if there were any messages. There were two unread messages from Jacob. She clicked on the 'message icon' to check, *"Good morning Jill. I liked the concept but it still need some changes. Hope to discuss with you in office"*. Reading this text, Jill's expressions changed. Furrowed eye brows. Narrowed eyes. Clenched Jaw. "What is this? I have written the best I could", she said to herself and started typing *"I won't come today. Don't text me"* which she backspaced immediately after a second.

"Jill, calm down. It is just the job", she said to herself and typed "Ok, Sir. For today, I need a day off due to headache" and sent it. She left her phone on the bedside table and went into the washroom. "Macy, Laxie. They didn't wake up", she said and without any delay, came in the hall. "God, these girls", she climbed the stairs. She entered into Macy's room saying "Girls, wake up. It's past 9. Girls?" There was silence in the room, yet again. A shiver ran down her spine and her legs stopped moving because last night, she saw the girls sleeping on that bed. She straightaway removed the blanket from the bed and threw it on the floor.

"Macy, Laxie", she yelled at the peak of her voice. She threw the pillow on the side wall. "This is driving me crazy!" she said in a strained voice. "Macy! Laxie, come here", she said while clenching her fists. After a minute, she opened the bathroom door and entered inside to check. "Macy! Macy where are you?" she said while her eyes started to turn red due to anger. Her emotions got heightened and build up to hit her suddenly. "Are they taking any revenge by hiding? Macy! Laxie! Come out" she warned. After getting tired of searching, her anger turned into sadness. Her eyes were puffy and swollen from crying. She came downstairs and shouted their names from the hall, "Macy! Laxie!" She kept her hand on the forehead and surrendered on the floor. "I don't know what to do. Macy! Laxi..laxie", she bellowed while bending her face forward. Few seconds later, she fainted and lost her consciousness.

Couple of minutes passed, Jill experienced some droplets of water on her face. Small hands touching her face continuously. She slowly opened her eyes and her vision was blurry. There were two faces gazing at her. She started blinking excessively to clear the clouds that were covering her eyes and when the vision got back to normal, she saw Laxie and Macy near her. She immediately used her hands to push herself up, and sat down with the crossed legs. Due to the fall, she was slightly feeling disoriented about her surroundings and after regaining the entire state of mind, she asked "La..Macy...Where were you? I was looking for you both". The tears started to roll out of her eyes while speaking.

Macy wiped her tears and said "Don't cry, Mommy. We were just playing hide and seek". Jill held Macy's hand and questioned "With me?" Hearing this, Macy and Laxie started looking at each other and Macy replied, "We were sad about yesterday and that's why hid in the closet". Jill was absolutely flabbergasted when she found out about the closet thing. "Closet? Seriously? It is not ventilated and can lead to dizziness or short..shortness of breath", Jill said while throwing her hands in the air. Macy and Laxie kept their eyes down while their mother was throwing out the words in panic. "We are sorry", both said in unison while looking at each other. "We didn't mean to cause you the problem", Macy continued. "But this really did hurt me. Why do you always behave like this?" Jill said while folding her hands around her bust and broke the eye contact. "Mommy, we are extremely sorry", Macy touched her mother's chin to shift her face to make an eye contact. "You regularly do this to me even though I treat you the best any mother could", she replied while wrinkles spread on her forehead. "Mom, we are sorry", Laxie said. Jill nodded her head and three of them stood up. Because of the incident, Jill's thoughts were racing inside and outside her head. She wanted to scream and throw away the things. She even missed to wash her face after waking up that morning and knew something was off around her. "Room?" she remembered. Leaving Macy and Laxie in the hall, she rushed to Macy's room. The space was disturbed. Before fainting, when she was searching for the girls, she scattered everything haphazardly in anger. The decorative vase had been knocked over, spilling the water and flowers on the floor. The books on the study table were a mess. The rug earlier centered in the middle of the room was shifted to one side, revealing the bare floor underneath. The blanket was near the wall, pillows thrown away in the different corners of the room. Overall, the room looked like a complete chaos. Her mouth was agape with guiltiness. "What did I do?" she said to herself while picking the pieces of vase from the floor.

Following her, Macy and Laxie reached into the room. "Girls..Girls I am so sorry", Jill said while taking the blame on herself. She moved her fingers in the hair and explained "I didn't mean to..didn't mean to", she said and started arranging the room. "Do not enter barefoot. You will hurt yourselves", Jill said and places all the pieces in one corner. "We too are sorry, Mommy. We made you angry", Laxie said while facing downwards. Jill's entire concentration was on the disorientation of the room. She quickly started to place the things as they were and collected debris in the corner. She picked the left behinds and went downstairs to throw in the dustbin. "We are sorry, Mommy", Laxie and Macy repeated. "It's okay. Mistakes happen", Jill replied. "Now, give me five minutes. I'll go and come back quickly", she continued and entered into her room then her washroom. Later on, she got ready and came outside. Macy and Laxie were playing while sitting on the floor. "Let me get my doll house", Macy said got it from her room. "Bring the doll dresses too", Laxie said in a loud voice. Macy replied "Yes" from her room. Jill saw this and smiled, went to check the sticks in the furnace. "It's too cold today", she said. "Laxie, ain't you feeling cold?" she continued speaking. "No", replied Laxie.

"Tell me, what you want to eat today?" she asked while inspecting if there were any seals in the ductwork. "Not hungry", Laxie replied. "You are not hungry?" Jill questioned in a surprise. "You both haven't eaten from last night", she continued. "I know but my tummy feels full", Laxie said. "No, we are going to take something in the breakfast. Well we have left the breakfast timings a lot behind", she continued speaking while looking at the clock. "I will quickly make omelet with cheddar cheese", Jill said. "Okay, Mommy", Laxie sighed.

Meanwhile, Macy came and sat near Laxie. Jill repeated the breakfast menu and went inside the kitchen. She took out cheddar cheese and placed it in a cup. After opening the cupboard, she took out the bowl and kept it on the slab. She picked five eggs from the egg carrot and placed them carefully in the bowl. Macy came running towards her and asked "Mommy, aren't you late for your office today?" to which Jill replied "No, because I have taken today's off". Macy surprisingly said "Oh" and went back to Laxie. Jill smiled and shifted back her attention on the eggs.

While she was picking the knife, she started experiencing a

severe pain at the backside of her head. Her sensitivity to light increased and she started feeling nauseated. She placed her left hand on the slab to provide a support to her body. "What is happening?" she said to herself, and after a few seconds, everything returned to normal. Her eyes stopped paining, there was no feeling of sickness, and her surrounding turned back to usual. "What just happened?" she said to herself.

She looked at Macy and Laxie to validate the normalcy. The thoughts which flushed off her mind, a while ago, came running back to her. She started questioning everything that was happening with her from the last night and times before. She thought of calling Matt but stopped herself instantly. "Matt will be worried", she murmured and continued doing her work. While picking the garlic, her hands kept shaking subtly and voice had a soft trembling, "Macy..please bring my phone". Macy looked at her and asked "Where is it?" Jill pointed her index finger towards her bedroom and said "My room".

Macy stood up and ran inside her parents' bedroom and searched for the mobile phone. She picked it from the bedside table and came running towards her mother. Jill unlocked the phone and checked the notifications. "Three missed calls from Matt", she exclaimed. She quickly dialed his number but the network was not reachable. "Matt, where are you?" she said. After trying multiple times, she kept the phone on the oven and turned her head towards the bowl. She cracked the eggs in the bowl one by one and added the milk in it. She whisked the eggs until well blended, slightly frothy and then seasoned it with a pinch of salt and pepper.

At the same time, her phone started to ring. "Matt, Matt", she dropped the spoon on the floor in a hurry. She picked her phone to answer, it was from him. "Matt? Hello?" she answered the phone call. "Hello, where are you?" he questioned with a clear panic in his voice. "I called you several times", he continued speaking. Jill took a pause and thought of telling him about what all happened with her since morning but she stopped herself and collected all her calmness to answer. "I..I was in the..washroom and when.. when I called you back, your.. your phone was not reachable", she said while trying to hide her emotions. "Okay!" he said after an intense thought. "I called to check upon you. Had shower? How do you feel now?" he spoke. Jill kept her hand over his neck and replied "All good. Making cheeeeeeeeeeese omelette". Matt's smile was clearly visible through the phone. "I feel great after hearing this. Hope to see you happy like this always", he answered. She exchanged love over the phone, disconnected the call and kept the phone handy in case he calls again.

The conversation and the different ways she could have used to convey her feelings were roaming inside her head from left to right. "I could have told him about..", she said and tried to divert her mind by continuing the work. Jill turned on the gas to heat the skillet and poured the mixture in the skillet and adjusted the required flame. "Macy, Laxie. Take your chairs. I have prepared your plates. She took the plates and kept it on the table. Both of them sat facing each other and picked the plates one by one. "Ketchup? Macy asked Laxie. "Yuck", Laxie gave a disgusting expression. "I mean why not? I love it!" Macy exclaimed. "Mommy, serve us the ketchup please", said Macy while teasing Laxie. "Why us? You need it. Take it on your name", said Laxie. "Stop fighting, girls! Take this", Jill said while giving the bowl to Macy.

"I overheard that you were not hungry", said Macy with the eyebrows raised. "Eavesdropper", replied Laxie. Without giving any answer to it, Macy shifted her focus back to the omelette. "Yum mum", she said. "You copied my words. I used to tell mom, yum-mum", Laxie responded. Hearing this Jill asked, "What is happening, girls? Why are you two fighting again?" Macy and Laxie stopped speaking and looked at their plates. Jill brought two more omelettes in the extra plate to serve each to them, "Come on, one more to go!" she said. "Mommy, I am full this time", said Laxie. "Same", replied Macy. "One more. It will finish in two bites", said Jill while trying to put one-one into their plates. "No!" said Laxie and jumped out of her chair. Jill looked at both of them and entered back into the kitchen saying "Wash your hands before you touch anything. And Macy, your cheeks are dipped in ketchup, go and wash them."

Jill kept the extra plate on the slab and placed the dirty plates in the sink. "I should eat something too. Feeling dizzy already!" she said while looking at the time. "How come Jacob hasn't replied yet. Hasn't he approved my leave?" she murmured and took the plate in one hand, the phone in other. She sat on the dining table and started scrolling down the messages on her phone. "Ayra didn't come yet", she said and took a bite of cheese omelette. "It tastes good but I need the cheese dip", saying this, she entered back to the kitchen and opened the fridge. "Opening this fridge feels like I am taking snow in my warm hands", she said while feeling the air coming out of the fridge on her cheeks. "Cheese dip, cheese..here it is", she mumbled and took it out.

While she was taking another bite from her **omelette**, there was a sudden thud sound from the under of the dining table on which she was sitting. Jill was astonished and her eyes immediately started searching for the girls, thinking they might be under it to scare her. To her surprise, Macy and Laxie were coming out of the store room, seen discussing about something only they knew. She was so afraid to bend down and check that she passed the thought naming it under 'Normal' thing. There was again a thud sound and this time louder than before, she now folded her legs and shifted at the back of her chair. With all the courage she had in her body, she shifted the plate away from her and slightly bent. She shut her eyes before bending down completely in order to save herself from a shock and later opened her eyes. She was even more shocked to find nothing in front of her eyes. While looking at the back side of the table, she blinked her eyes for several times.

Jill started sweating and her emotions were swirled. "How ca.." she was about to complete the words but before that Macy tapped her on her shoulder. She screamed out loud saying "Stay away from me". Macy was looking at her with the mixed expressions on her face. "Mom, what happened?" Macy asked. She took a minute to even move her lips and was failing to understand the situation. Even worse, how to say it, "Nothing, sweety! Nothing! Aaaaaaaaaa. You scared me!" Jill replied in a very dramatic tone to make Macy laugh but Macy didn't. "Mommy, you feel seriously scared", Macy said while Laxie joined them. "What is going on?" asked Laxie. "Mommy, why haven't you completed even a single **omelette** on your plate?" Laxie pretended as if she was interrogating. "Because Mommy screamed when I touched her", Macy said. "I think she is scared", Macy whispered this statement in Laxie's ears. Now both the girls started staring at Jill and sweat was not leaving Jill's forehead at all. She quickly shifted her face towards the plate and started eating. "Mommy", Laxie said. "Macy, Laxie. Go and play!" Jill said. Both the girls faced each other and then after waiting for few seconds, resumed playing. Jill was watching them from the corner of her eyes, trying to avoid the last fifteen minutes. She chomped from the plate and went in the kitchen to place it on the slab. She started moving her hands at full tilt to avoid the overcrowded thoughts. "What was that sound?" she said to herself and instantly picked her phone to inform Matt. She scrolled down the messages and texted him *"Matt, Please call me whenever you have time"* and sent it. She kept looking at the message, hoping for an immediate response and couldn't stop herself from feeling anxious so she called him. The phone rang till the last ring but there was no response. She knew somewhere in her heart that he was busy but her emotions overpowered her mental ability to think. She kept dialling Matt's number but all the calls went unanswered.

"What is with you, Matt?" Jill said while looking at her phone. After exhausting mentally, she left the phone on the kitchen slab and went inside her room. "Everything's a mess, everyone test me!" Jill said to herself while standing in front of the mirror. "There's no sign of Jimmy. She hasn't even bothered to call back. Matt is not answering my phone. Macy and Laxie test my patience at my lowest. I am tired. Nobody is understanding what is happening with me. I am seeing and feeling weird things. I am sick of it", she broke down and sat on the floor. There was a mixture of sadness and anger in her eyes. She kept crying and in some moment, she thought of Macy and Laxie. So, she put her hand on her face to prevent them from seeing her cry.

A melancholy mood washed over her face as she watched herself in the mirror. She wiped her tears, went inside the washroom, opened the tap and kept splashing the water on her face. The bathroom mirror fogged with the warmth of her heavy breaths. It felt like Jill's reflection was staring her back. With immense tiredness and confusion on her face, it felt like dark smoke was settled under her eyes. Cupping her hands, she kept splashing the water onto her face. Water trickled down her neck, smoothly, softly. She took a deep breath, the world then seemed less blurry because all that was pricking her in the heart a minute before, later beaded on her skin. The mirror was now clear, dampened hair touched her neck and shoulder.

She took out the face towel from her almirah and dabbed at her face. After hanging the towel on the door hangers, she said "I should clean this mess" and went out of her room. She saw the girls once and then entered the store room and picked the vacuum cleaner to started cleaning. "Girls, please arrange your things. I am cleaning now", Jill said and overlapped the vacuum path. Macy and Laxie started chasing each other from one room to another. "Girls, please. I am cleaning", Jill screamed on the top of her voice, reaching to their ears by breaking through the vacuum sound.

Jill was checking the dust bag and her eyes caught attention on a printed photograph that was partially burnt. She took it out from the bag to take a closer look. "What is this?" she said. The intense heat from the fire destroyed the image beyond repair and there was just a wall and a head visible in it. After spending much time on it, she realized what she was doing. "Macy, where are your socks?" Jill said while looking at the girls. "And Laxie, please, I am cleaning the hall. Please play somewhere else", Jill continued speaking while empting the dirt bag. She kept the burnt picture on the table and carried on doing her work.

"Macy, do you think we will ever grow old?" asked Laxie. "No", Macy replied laughingly. "Can I make your ponytail?" Laxie questioned Macy. "No", Macy responded with a laughter. "I won't talk to you now", Laxie said while stomping her feet. "You won't play with me? Then I will throw all your toys on the floor", said Macy to continue the pity fight. "Do not touch them. I am going to tell mom about it", said Laxie while shielding her toys. Jill was seeing all this and somehow she felt happy seeing them grow old together.

Macy and Laxie used to make Jill's gloomy day into a happening one. She always loved to stay around them. Her heart was always open with love whenever she thought of them. "No, no don't touch me", said Laxie and rushed to wrap her hands around Jill's waist. "She is mine and we don't know you", she continued speaking. "Mommy, she was teasing me!" Macy complained. "I know! I know!" replied Jill while throwing her hands in the air and neck movement in left and right direction. "By the way, we are going for a party tomorrow", said Jill while holding Laxie from her shoulders. "Aunt Ayra has invited us", she continued speaking and later sat on her knees.

Her phone started to ring. "It must be Matt", she said and rushed to pick her phone.

"Boss?" she said and immediately swiped right to answer the phone. "Hello?" he said. "Good afternoon, Boss", she replied. "Jill, we want to publish your article but some changes are yet to be done", he spoke. Jill was listening to him silently. "Are you available for an hour?" he questioned. Jill looked at the girls and answered, "Actually, I am not well". It wasn't a lie because after every hour or two, she felt crippling pain at the back of her head. Jacob stayed quiet and then continued speaking, "Okay. We are left with no choices but to publish this article next year. Good day!" he said and disconnected the call. Jacob's tone was bitter and Jill could feel the heat on the phone call. "How inhumane", she said while looking at her phone.

"Come on girls, let's click a picture", she said to lighten the environment and forget what mess turned her understanding upside down. Macy and Laxie came running towards her and tilted their faces on either sides. "Say cheese!" Jill said. "Cheese? I will say 'smile please'", Macy said. They clicked a picture and Jill looked at her with a biggest grin. "We love you, Mommy", Macy and Laxie said while kissing Jill's cheeks. "I am blessed!" said Jill while touching her jugular notch.

"Speaking of which, where do you girls hide to banter me?" Jill laughed while sipping the water from her glass. "A secret place", Macy whispered in Jill's ears. "The store room right?" Jill questioned. "Nope! That is just one of them", replied Laxie while winking at Macy. Jill was eager to know about the places, so she could find them the next time. "Mommy, can we please go out today?" asked Macy. "Why do you want to go out?"

Laxie frowned. "So that we can have quality time", replied Macy. "Ain't we having special time?" asked Jill. "Not without father", said Macy while making a duck face. "Aw. Come here", Jill opened her arms while adoring them. "Hey, why are you crying Laxie?" questioned Jill. "Because we try so hard to keep you happy but hurt you some how", replied Laxie. "But girls, you are my happy place. Who said I am not happy with you?" Jill consoled. "Don't think this way, sweety. You make me laugh and cry which is a very good thing. It makes me feel alive and I am absolutely blessed to have you as my children", replied Jill while kissing Laxie's forehead. "Mine too", said Macy with a puppy eyes. "Come on now, go and take a shower. I will prepare a fresh meal for you and then we will go out to see the city. Eve's approaching, yayaye!" said Jill to cheer them up. "Can we now buy candies?" asked Macy. "And balloons too?" added Laxie. "You girls! Fooling me?" Jill mocked. "Noooooooooo!" replied the girls. "So, tell me. What do you want to eat? Look its 3 and we are already late for the lunch", said Jill. "Fish chips", said Laxie while raising her one hand. "Fish Soup", said Macy while raising both her hands. "Only one thing", said Jill. "Fish Chips", said Laxie while looking at Macy. "Okay!" Macy agreed. "Okay then, take your showers and you will find the chips ready", said Jill. Macy stepped on the stair and said "Mommy, orange juice as well" hearing which Jill nodded. "These girls absolutely love drinking juices", she said while smiling.

Jill went inside the kitchen and said "I can't eat this omelette and kept the plate near the sink". She opened the freezer and took out one. She started cutting the cod fillets into strips and took out one plate to combine the flour, salt and pepper. While dipping the strips in the mixture and in another bowl, she kept combining the eggs with few drops of water and later opened the drawer to take out the box of breadcrumbs and poured some on the strips. She kept the large skillet on the stove, poured some vegetable oil in it and kept the strips one by one. After heating each side for approximately 5 to 7 minutes until they turned golden brown, she picked the strips using tongs and kept on the plate. Later she sprinkled the salt and some sauce on it. "There you go!" she said to herself and kept the serving plates on the dining table. "Girls! Lunch is ready" she called.

She opened the freezer to take out the juice can. She placed two glasses on the slab and poured the juice in each and later kept it on the table. "Hm, I can quickly make a soup", she said to herself feeling overwhelmed to make children choose one out of two dishes. She rushed inside the kitchen and instantly took out a large pot. After keeping the pot over medium heat, she poured some olive oil. "Let me quickly chop some veggies", she said and took out carrots, onions, garlic from the basket. She added the vegetables in the pot and left them to cook for 5 minutes. She then added the fish broth and stirred it while adding leaves, celery, diced tomatoes. While taking out the fish fillets and added them in the pot while bringing the heat to simmer, she added the salt and pepper in it. "Ready!" she said and kept the bowl on the table after garnishing with parsley.

"Girls!" Jill repeated and went upstairs. She knocked Macy's door and went inside. Macy was nowhere visible. She immediately went inside Laxie's room unannounced. "Laxie, Macy. Taken shower? Come now", she said and opened the bathroom door. Unexpectedly for her, the bathroom was empty. "To her wonder, the girls were not there. And this was second time in a day. Jill felt a growing sense of annoyance because this was literally making her feel crazy. "Girls! Enough of hiding. Please come out!" she said while coming downstairs. "I am not searching for any of you, just waiting on the dining table", she continued speaking.

Jill headed towards the dining table, pulled the chair to sit and started to drum nails on the table. She looked at the clock and realized Matt hadn't called her too. She picked her phone to check and saw a text message from him. "Jill, your phone isn't reachable. Please call me!" Jill read the message and kept the phone aside. Fifteen minutes passed like that but to her disbelief, the girls were still away from her eyes. Anxious she was, stood up and went into the store room. She turned on the lights and checked the corners. The girls weren't there. She later went inside her room, the balcony, back yard and even checked the main door which was locked from inside.

Jill alarmingly turned around and suddenly her eyes caught attention of a blue scarf which was visible from under the table. She immediately rushed to pick it up and started checking. "This is of Macy", she said to herself and ducked to check. The other end of the table was clearly visible. "Macy!" she said in a loud voice. "Come out children, Mommy is not feeling right", she said and went inside her bedroom. She turned on the lights, open her cupboards, entered into the bathroom, shifted the bathroom curtain and came out. "Girls, food is turning cold and this is not funny", Jill yelled. Her heart started racing faster, her palms were sweaty as she tried to steady her breathing. She stopped at the edge of her room, her face flushed and her eyes were wide with panic. She placed her finger around her nose and started calling them. "Macy, Laxie, where are you? Please come outside". Her hands were trembling and her mind started to whirl with worry. She began imagining the worst case scenarios: "Maybe they stepped outside the home when I was cooking or maybe they locked themselves somewhere and couldn't open the door or maybe they are injured and fainted". Her eyes scanned the entire place but there was no sign. Jill's throat tightened and she could barely swallow. "Girls! Where are you?" he voice cracked with desperation. She checked every where she could and wherever girls told her about their secret places. She sat down on the chair and looked at the clock. Her thoughts were a chaotic jumble but she clinged to the hope that the girls will appear any moment.

Minutes felt like hours, every passing moment without them made her panic worse but she resolved to keep hoping, determined not to give up until she find them. There was a thud sound again and that time from not under the table but from the main door. Jill felt herself began to swoon as she stood up instantly after hours of racing her mind. She quickly rushed to open the door but stopped near the door before opening. "Should I check from the window", she said and sneaked to take a look. She noticed a faint light coming from the corner of the street. As she moved her eyes on the left side, she was startled. There were the girls! Completely drenched in the water. Her heart started racing as she opened the door. The girls hugged her and started crying helplessly.

Jill failed to understand what exactly happened. "Girls! Girls!" she said in a loud voice. "How did you go out and what happened?" she continued speaking. The girls kept crying and the water kept falling from their hair. Their legs felt stiff from cold and their teeth were chattering. Jill took them inside, \em sit near the furnace and ran to bring their clothes.

"Change your clothes", she handed the clothes to them and started helping them in opening the buttons of the sweaters and pants. Jill's heart was pounding, her fingers started shivering while helping them in drying their hair. She immediately went in the kitchen to get the hot water to drink. The girls folded their legs and sat near the fire to the maximum extent. They were shivering uncontrollably.

Jill immediately brought the water and gave the glasses to each one of them. "Drink slowly. Sip by sip", she said and covered them with a blanket. "Now, tell me. How did you end up like this?" she questioned in a sympathetic voice. Macy and Laxie were looking at each other and took the sip of water before speaking anything. "Girls? Please tell me", Jill requested. "The door was closed, and I was in the kitchen the entire time. How di..I mean how did you go out?" Jill interrogated. Macy kept the glass on the floor and covered herself using the blanket, even hid the fingers. "Girls, are you listening?" she emphasized the words while speaking. "Mommy, we were playing an..", Macy started to speak. "But I sent you two to take bath", Jill put her point before Macy could complete her sentence. "And we were playing and we went into our rooms, our ball was kicked out of the window by Laxie and that was..that was by accident. So", Macy hesitated. "So?" Jill asked with her pale expressions on face. "Laxie..", Macy spoke and stopped. "Laxie? Laxie what?" Jill questioned and looked at Laxie. "Laxie you tell me. Laxie?" Jill commanded. "My leg slipped off the edge and I fell down. Macy was holding my hand and due to imbalance, she struggled too. Both of us rolled down from the clay tiles and ended up in the garden outside", Laxie said while keeping her eyes down at the floor. Jill was astonished. "You fell? And Macy you didn't even bother to call me?" she bombarded them with the sack of questions. "And moreover, you ended up out, in this extreme cold and rain?" she continued speaking with the slight redness in her eyes. If someone had kept a hand on her shoulder, she would have cried. "Did you get hurt?" she questioned while checking their hands and legs. "Are you bleeding from somewhere, tell me. Laxie, did you get hurt?" she kept questioning while keeping her hand over Laxie's chin. "Laxie, tell me girl!" she said while running her fingers behind her neck.

Laxie nodded. "I didn't but Macy did. She got a scratch on her leg", she confessed. Jill's eyes widened and she checked Macy's legs. It was her knee which was bleeding. She immediately got up, went in the store room and got the first aid box. She took out a band aid and opened it to stick on her knee. "Is it paining?" Jill questioned softly. Macy nodded in agreement saying "Not exactly but yes". "How are you both feeling now?" Jill questioned. "Better", said Laxie.

Jill took a deep breath and said "Macy, Laxie? When you need help, ask for it. Don't ever behave like this again". Macy and Laxie kept staring the floor without replying to it. "Come, we will have food. Everything is stale by now", Jill said in a subtle tone. All three of them went to the dining table and sat on the chairs. "Do you know I was so scared that I even started having nightmares during the broad daylight? I even searched for you both in every corner of the home but look at the situation, you were outside it", Jill started explaining. "Pick your plates", she diverted the topic and took the bowl in her hands. The girls placed their plates in front of them while hiding themselves under the blanket. "No air should enter inside", said Macy while looking at Laxie.

"Where is the dip?" asked Laxie. "Mommy it has turned cold. My soup", Macy said while pouting. "One second", Jill left her chair and went inside the kitchen. She turned on the oven switch and placed the bowl inside it. After setting the temperature, she opened the front drawer to pick out the packed dips. She took out a cup and poured some in it. The timer rang. She opened the oven door and took out the soup bowl.

"Take this", Jill placed the bowl in front of Macy. "For your finger chips", she continued moving around the table. "Here's the cheese dip and I am bringing the sauce as well", she said and opened the cap of sauce pouch. "It would have tasted good when served hot but no worries. We will have a new form of food today", she said while looking at Laxie. Macy took one sip of her soup and gave a satisfactory look. "Yum!" Macy said. Jill saw her and smiled. Laxie took the fish finger in her hand but looked confused. "What happened?" questioned Macy. "Shall I try it with cheese dip or sauce?" she questioned. "Go plain", Macy replied while taking another sip. "Avoid drinking the juice, Macy. Don't combine it with the liquid. In fact skip the juice for a while", she pointed towards the glasses while looking at the girls.

Right after saying the statement, she shifted the glasses on one side. "Girls, do you feel like eating anything else. I know today was hectic and has compromised our time table but it is absolutely okay to tell me", Jill said while expecting their attention on the table. "French fries", Laxie whispered. "Mommy, can we order something?" Macy questioned while finishing her soup. "But it's raining. Tell me, I will make it at home", Jill replied. "Vegetable Noodles", Laxie whispered again while picking the second last fish finger from the common bowl. "Something light", Macy said while looking at Laxie. "Corn pizza", Laxie said while looking at Jill. "We don't have corns", replied Jill while piling the empty plates. "Macaroni and cheese", said Macy. "Is this light?" asked Laxie while rolling her eyes.

"Don't give me that look. I fell to save you", said Macy while acting defensive. "We both were playing with the ball", argued Laxie. "Hey! Hey!" said Jill while cutting the air between them with her hand. "What happened suddenly?" she continued questioning. "Mac and cheese, right? We can eat that", said Jill while easing the tense environment. "Laxie, is it okay?" questioned Jill. "Add some veggies", Laxie instructed while nodding her head in agreement. "Veggies? It is plain", said Macy. "Girls, listen to me. We are making it right now. Come with me in the kitchen", said Jill while washing her hands.

After multiple bad incidents, she was not ready to leave the girls out of her sight. "Laxie, you will help me in boiling the macaroni and Macy, you'll grate the cheese. Got it?" Jill handed over the major responsibilities to them. Jill opened the kitchen almirah to take out the packet of elbow macaroni. She later opened the fridge to take the butter, cold milk, cheddar cheese, tomatoes and bell peppers out of it. After keeping all the items on the slab, she opened the middle drawer under the slab and took out black pepper, garlic powder and flour. "Oh I forgot to take out the cream. Macy, open the fridge and took out the can of fresh cream", Jill said while looking at Macy.

As instructed, Macy picked the can and gave it to Jill. "Perfect! We have all the items available", said Jill. The girls started to jump in excitement. "We are learning how to cook", Laxie said while adjusting her blanket. "Just because we are working in the kitchen and temperature has got back to normal, please keep this blanket outside. It may catch fire", said Jill while keeping the large pot of water to boil. She sprinkled some salt in it. "Laxie, add the macaroni in it", Jill said while giving the container to Laxie. "As per instructions, Laxie poured the quantity inside the water. Jill checked it and started chopping the vegetables. "Pass me the onion from the basket", said Jill to Laxie. She handed over the two onions to Jill and questioned, "Mommy, can I sit on the slab? I will be able to see it better". Jill looked her from the side of her eyes and replied "Only from a distance". Laxie jumped to sit on the slab and started watching her cook. "Macy, please take the cheese block and grate it. Take this bowl as well and do not spill or get hurt", Jill said while pointing her direction towards the cheese. Macy nodded her head, took the block and cheese grater. Jill checked the pot and the condition of macaroni. After feeling satisfied, she drained the water of macaroni, poured them on the plate and kept it aside. She later placed the saucepan at medium heat and put some butter in it. After it melted, she whisked the flour and cooked it for over a minute and kept stirring constantly. The bubbles started to form and mixture turned light golden. She later whisked the milk in it and cream. The mixture started to turn thick after five minutes. "Macy, done?" Jill questioned while expecting the bowl of cheese ready in her hands. "A minute, Mommy", Macy requested and later gave the bowl to Jill. She reduced the heat to low, added the shredded cheese and kept stirring until the cheese melted in a fine ratio. Later added all the vegetables inside it and kept stirring. Seasoning it with salt, pepper and garlic powder. "Do we have chilli flakes?" Laxie questioned. "Yes, do you want me to add it?" asked Jill while focusing on the pan. "Yes, but Macy avoids eating it", Laxie replied while looking at Macy.

"Mommy, don't add it", requested Macy. "Okay, Darling", Jill said. "How is your leg now?" Jill questioned. "Better", Macy replied while looking at her mother's hands. "I am so craving to eat it", she continued speaking. "Almost ready", Jill replied while touching Macy's head. Jill preheated the oven to approximately 190 degree Celsius. She combined the cheese sauce with the macaroni until pasta was evenly coated. After pouring the macaroni in baking dish, she kept it inside the oven and shut its door. While keeping her eyes on the oven, Jill questioned "So, tell me girls. How do you want to celebrate New Year?" Macy and Laxie whispered something in each other's ears and replied "Nothing. Just surprise gifts". "Smart!" Jill responded. The sauce started to turn bubbly and the outer structure was visibly golden brown. Jill wore oven mitts and opened the oven door. "Laxie, get off the slab now. I need to keep it there", Jill instructed and picked the container and kept it on the slab. Macy started jumping while her hands were raised high. "Looks yum!" Laxie commented. "Because the girls helped me in making it", Jill credited them. "Let it cool. Grab your forks", said Jill. Macy took out three spoons from the spoon stand and distributed them. After ten minutes of discussion, she took the baking dish and kept it on the dining table while removing the mitts. "Jump in", Jill said in an exciting voice.

Three of them put their forks and started eating. "Slowly, let it cool before you place it over your tongue", Jill instructed. "Mommy, this is the best", said Laxie. "Veggies are making the macaroni even more delicious", she continued speaking. "I never thought of this combination before but it has really surprised me", said Macy while moving her mouth. "I feel full", said Jill while rubbing her hand over her stomach. "I am not", said Macy. "I can eat this for life", she commented. Jill grinned while putting her fork in the cheese. "I love cheese", Jill said. "Really", said Laxie. "The melted one obviously", Jill added. There was laughter and contentment in the room. "Ready for the juice, now?" questioned Jill. "Yes", replied Macy. "Definitely!" added Laxie. Jill gave the glasses to both the girls and took the empty dish inside the kitchen. "Mommy, where is your glass?" questioned Macy. "I have no space in my tummy. I will take it later", Jill replied. "By the way, do I need to consider your episode with rain as your actual cleaning? As much as I know, you both skipped bathing", Jill questioned while wiping the slab with the cloth. The girls avoided her question and kept their focus on finishing the juice glasses. "Loved the meal!" Laxie said while changing the topic and placing the glass near the sink. "Yeah, right!" exclaimed Jill.

After a good rain, it started to snow. The hall was warm but the rooms, they turned slightly cold. It was a pleasant evening, and three of them had an emotional ups and downs since they woke up. Jill decided to call back Matt which she left on hold because of inner turmoil. She picked her phone, scrolled her call logs. "Matt, Matt, Matt, ah here it is", she said and clicked on the name followed by the call icon. Matt answered her phone in the fifth ring with a gasp and said, "Hello?" Hearing his voice, Jill's expressions changed and she questioned, "What happened?" Matt instantly threw questions saying "You tell me? What is going on? Why didn't you answer the phone? And one second, where are you? Are you safe? Are you okay? Again had bad dreams?"

Matt kept on speaking and Jill's wrinkles on the forehead, slowly vanished. "Hey! Hey! Hey!" she spoke to give it a rest. "I am okay. Safe. At home. Waiting for you. No nightmares", she continued explaining by adding the breaks after every answer.

"Then…Then why so many calls? What happened? And why didn't you pick your phone later?" After hearing this, Jill took a pause before speaking to carefully choose her words and ensure she communicated her thoughts clearly. "First of all, tell me where you are?" she questioned. "I am leaving the office in a minute. I had a little panic attack when you dodged my calls", he replied while picking his bag and the car keys from the table. "Then you were supposed to come at that time only. Why waited for three long hours?" she questioned. "Wow", he said while smirking. "Chill, I am just teasing. Come home, we will have a nice conversation and I will definitely explain what all happened in the last twelve hours", she said. He exchanged goodbyes with her by moving his index finger from his forehead to the air. Jill kept the phone on the table and started to arrange the slipcovers of the sofa set while dusting the surface of sofa. She had a smile on her face remembering her best times with the girls.

"Ayra didn't come", she reminded herself and picked her phone to call her. She missed the first call but Jill redialled her number. After second ring, Ayra said "Hi!" Jill replied with a smile "Hey! You didn't come". Ayra's face expressions changed and she replied with furrowed eyebrows, "I did". "You did?" Jill repeated after her with a tensed expression on her forehead. "Yes! Infact Liam came too. We even called you but the phone was switched off", Ayra tried to convince her by explaining the situation. "But.." Jill tried to defend herself. "And we even rang the bell but since there was no response. We knocked the door and later without any response, left the place", Ayra explained. "Oh, Okay. I must be somewhere far from the main door. It was totally unintentional", Jill said with a flushed face. "No..No..worries. No formalities, come tomorrow! Okay?" Ayra responded with an expectation to receive a nod from the other side of the phone. With an unnatural smile, Jill replied

"Yes, yes!" and disconnected the call.

Jill ran a hand through her hair and started staring at the wall. "What just happened?" she questioned and decided to discuss it with Matt. Macy came near Jill with her band aid half peeled. "What happened?" Jill questioned and sat on her knees to take a closure look. "We were playing and this suddenly came off", Macy said while pointing towards her leg. "Because the sticky part is not sticky anymore", Jill said with a smile. "Okay, now shut your eyes. I am going to remove this very quickly", she said while moving her finger over the band aid. "Is it going to hurt?" Macy questioned while closing her eyes dramatically. "One. Two. And go", Jill counted and took the band aid off her knee. Macy was standing while holding her breath. "It was supposed to be three after two", informed Macy. "But in our case, it's a go", Jill mockingly laughed. "Now go and play. You're absolutely fine", Jill directed. Macy ran towards the stairs and turned to ask in between, "Mommy, can we take the packet of chips and soft drink". "We?" Jill questioned. "I and Laxie want it, Mommy", Macy replied. "We have no soft drinks in our fridge. And chips…", Jill spoke and got disrupted by Macy's expressions. "We do have chips and soft drinks are hidden in the top cabinet", she said while keeping her hands on her waist. Cute!

"Okay, you'll kill your hunger if you eat at this hour", said Jill to convince Macy. "We want to eat it, Mommy", said Laxie while coming downstairs. "Look, Macy got hurt and she needs princess treatment", Laxie added to her statement while showing Macy's leg to her mom. "Cheaters!" said Jill while slightly tilting her neck on the left side. She opened the cabinet, took out a large sized bottle. "Woah", Macy exclaimed. "I didn't know we had it in stock", said Laxie. "One glass each", she said while raising her index finger in the air. Macy and Laxie nodded their heads and went near the slab. Macy took the glass and took a sip. "I think we should add ice too", said Laxie. "In this cold? Do you know what temperature is outside?" Jill questioned. "So, no ice!" Jill continued speaking. She then bent and opened the middle drawer under the slab, took out the box of wafers and presented it like a trophy. "Cheers!" Macy and Laxie clinked their glasses and picked the baskets from the box.

"This is my flavour", Laxie jumped while pointing at the packet. "And this mine", said Macy while touching the packet to her bust. "Okay now! Go and enjoy. Let me do my work", said Jill while putting the lid over the box. Both the girls took their glasses and chips in their hands. Jill put back the box on its place and shut the door. She later went near the window and removed the curtains. The weather was looking amazing. The air seemed heavy with moisture, and a chill could have seeped into the bones. Leaves, branches swayed in the wind and puddles were visible on the ground. "Cozy blankets, warm drinks and a good book. Perfect combination", Jill whispered while gently wrapping her arms around the shoulders.

She opened the bookcase and took out the book. "Ah! Left in between", she said to herself while taking out the bookmark and kept it above the bookcase. She held the book and went in the balcony. While sitting on the hammock, she looked around the balcony with a smile on her face. It felt like rain was about to fall on the ground. "We still have sometime", she said while facing her book. A gentle breeze carried the sweet scent of blooming wildflowers as she sat near the edge of her hammock. She closed her eyes and breathed deeply, took the serene beauty of the environment. "Blessed!" she exclaimed. A contended smile spread on her face as she savoured the moment of tranquillity. Jill was so drowned in the depth of serenity that she forgot to take a check on her surroundings. She didn't even turn a page to read the book so she took it in her hands, stood up and went inside the hall.

"Macy, Laxie, Where are you?" Jill said. Macy was in the lobby, near the main door and Laxie was braiding the doll's hair while sitting on the first stair. "Darling", Jill said. "Mommy, I want the candies", Laxie made an eye contact with Jill. "I knew it! Some demand's on the way", said Jill. "Please!" Laxie let her eyes reflect the emotions. It seemed as if Laxie was so passionate about what she was saying. "Okay! Okay", said Jill while showing her palm. "Macy, come here", said Jill. "What were you doing there?" she continued speaking. "I wish to paint the side walls", said Macy. "Okay!" Jill replied while emphasizing the word. "But you don't know how to do it", she spoke. "I know, Mum. But I will try. Plus, Laxie will help me too", said Macy. "We will give you a surprise on New Year. So you are not allowed to come in the lobby", defended Laxie. "But that's the only route to the main door", Jill said while positioning her with fingers slightly apart.
"You will buy us some colours", said Macy. "Okay, we will talk about it later", Jill said while hoping to postpone the discussion. "Eve's tomorrow. So we need colours in the morning, Mommy", Macy said while running towards the window. She looked outside and said "Snow has started. Mommy, please. Tomorrow!" Jill looked towards Laxie and she was standing while her hands joined. "Mommy, Please", Laxie pleaded. Jill nodded her head and smiled. "Okay, now tell me what we can have in our dinner", asked Jill. "Nothing, Mom. I am stuffed", said Macy. "Mommy, me too. I think I have overeaten", said Laxie. "Only wafers made you full?"

questioned Jill. "Mac hasn't digested yet", Laxie scorned. "Mommy, please give me the water in my sipper", said Macy. Jill nodded saying "Girls, you have started skipping your dinners and this is not a good thing" to which Laxie replied, "Mommy you only told us to not overeat. It will burst our small tummy". Jill was amazed to hear her point. "That statement was for junk", she said while filling the water in Macy's sipper.

"Mommy, we didn't decorate our Christmas tree this year", said Laxie. "Because daddy promised to bring the tree at home and he forgot", replied Jill while rolling her eyes. "And that is why we had to go out in order to decorate because tree was out of stock that day", said Macy. "How do you know?" questioned Laxie while keeping her hand on near the waist. "You didn't listen to their conversation?" asked Macy. "You were listening?" Jill said suspiciously. "No, No..Mo..mmy", Macy stammered. "I just heard", replied Macy. "Okay, now we are going in our rooms to prepare the designs for tomorrow with the spare colours I have", Macy continued speaking to dodge the conversation. Both the girls ran towards their rooms. "Hey! Stop", said Jill. The girls quickly climbed the stairs and went inside Macy's room.

Jill beamed and poured the milk in her mug. "I prefer it hot", she said while placing the microwave-safe container with milk in the microwave. She heated the milk on medium power by setting the temperature. After testing a small amount on her wrist, she poured the milk back into the mug. "Vanilla powder will add stars to the taste", she said while mixing it well. She took a sip out of it and kept her hand near her cheek while saying "Heaven!"

Day went well in Jill's life and she checked the time. It was

08:02 PM and the sun was resting somewhere out in the universe. "This weather has literally ceased my church trips. God, please forgive me", she said while crossing her fingers and looking at the ceiling as if it was allowing the way to the sky. She was enjoying a leisurely walk through the hall, savouring the coldness in the weather and drinking the milk sip by sip. To enhance her surroundings, there were elegant wall sconces on either side of the hall which were lit and highlighted the rich texture of the wallpaper. "Complete", she said while trying to seize everything that was near her. She kept the mug near the sink and took a sip of water to sustain the taste of flavour on her tongue. "Matt hasn't called yet", she said while looking at the main door. "I feel hungry", she murmured. She took her phone and redialled Matt's number. After two calls, Matt called her back. "Hello Yobo?" Jill was taken aback after hearing his voice. "Babe, I am so sorry! I couldn't answer you call. I was so occupied in all the meetings..", Matt kept on speaking. "Ishh.Ishh. I understood. I have called you to ask about the time you will take to reach here. I am controlling my hunger a lot", she replied while raising her bushy brows. "I will be late, darling. I am really sorry. I should have informed you earlier but believe me, I just got to know about the meeting that scheduled post 11. International client", Matt defended his position to which Jill nodded her head slowly. She kept her lips tightly zipped for a minute. "Hello?" said Matt to recheck if Jill was listening. "Yeah. Okay", replied Jill while resisting herself from wanting him to come back home then and there. "Babe. Just be safe. Stay Inside. I will be back till 12. Okay?" said Matt while waiting for her response. "And eat well. I will too grab a wrap quickly", he continued speaking. "Okay!" Jill replied with a wry smile. "I know you are not happy and we should not eat dinners without each other but believe me, baby. I will make up for it", replied Matt. "Okay. Love you!" said Jill with mixed emotions visible in her eyes.

She kept the phone and started thinking about every possible thing she could eat at that moment. "Um, I don't feel like cooking. Shall I order something?" she said to herself while looking outside the window. "Its 08:30 PM and restaurants must be open", she folded her hands while speaking. "What about Pizza?" she spoke while picking her phone and dialling the number of the nearby restaurant.

After two rings, a man answered the phone "Hello, this is 'Amicables'. What would you like to order?" to which Jill replied "Ah, yeah. Hi. This is Jill speaking, I would like to order a few things", Jill replied modestly. "One second", she said and put her phone on hold. "Girls! Macy and Laxie!" she called their names while looking towards the staircase. "Yes, Mommy", replied Macy and looked downwards. "Do you feel like eating something? I am ordering pizza for myself", Jill replied with a smile. "Oh, Plain Puffs for me. Laxie, do you want to add on something, Mom's ordering food?" Macy stated. "Nope! Full", replied Laxie from the room. "No, Mom. Just my order", said Macy and went back in her room. Jill took the phone off hold and said "Hi. I am sorry to make you wait. Please note the items. One Quattro Stagioni Pizza. Umm, One Plain Puff, One cheese quesadilla, like add more cheese to it and..umm..that's it. And oh, can you please list down the options in toppings?" A meek voice came from the other side of the phone, "We have Ham, Mushrooms, Olives and Tomatoes" to which Jill replied "Please replace olives with onions". She disconnected the call after confirming the order. She went inside her room and opened her almirah, took out the towel and the bathrobe. After entering the bathroom, she locked the door and removed the bathroom curtain, "I can take a quick shower before the delivery boy comes". Entering into the bath tub, she opened the faucet and let it run. Meanwhile, she used the bath sponge with a soap and cleaned her arms. "I should have informed the girls to keep their eyes on the door", she whispered and immediately rinsed off under the faucet. Using the towel, she gently pat the body dry. She wore the bath robe and came to her room. Slightly opening the door, she peeped outside to take a glance at the main door and later at the clock. "Five minutes remaining", she spoke softly. The moment she was thinking all of this, the doorbell rang and her mouth was left open. She ran towards the door and looked out from the peephole. A man wearing the cap and red jacket was standing in the doorway. Jill opened the door and took the parcel while handing over the money to him. "Thank you", both expressed gratitude. She shut the door and locked it. "Macy! The food's on the table", Jill announced and went back in her room. Her teeth were clattering, she speedily wore her night dress and left the robe on the bed. "I am feeling empty", she said and sat on the table. "Macy, your puff is getting cold. Come fast, bring Laxie along", Jill stated while opening the delivery bag. Macy came with her doll in the hands, pulled out a chair and sat in front of Jill. "Mommy, what have you got?" Macy asked. Jill was looking in the bag and replied "We have Pizza and quesadilla".

Macy clapped her hands in excitement and asked Jill to serve the pizza slice to her as well. Jill smiled while setting the plates and questioned, "Okay, Why didn't Laxie come?" Macy looked at her and replied "Because she is feeling sleepy in fact she has already slept". Jill lifted the pizza box and placed a slice in Macy's plate. "We have some sachets of chili flakes, garlic salt and basils", said Jill while moving the pizza box on the left side.

"Pass me a fresh plate, I will take out quesadilla in it", she continued speaking. "Mommy, can I take a bite from it?" asked Macy. "Sure, darling! It's all ours", replied Jill. "Delicious", said Macy. "We should often order our food from outside", Macy commented. "Why? Don't I make good one?" Jill questioned.

Both of them finished the food, "I am so full, Mommy. Please drop me to my room", said Macy while resting her shoulder on the top of backrest and head in the air. "Sweetie, go wash your hands fast", Jill said while arranging the plates on the table. She kept the stack near the sink and rinsed her mouth. "I am definitely missing Jimmy. I wonder where she is. Her son isn't picking the call as well, Infact he hasn't even replied to my calls", Jill murmured. Macy went inside her room and left her doll on the chair. "I have lots and lots of work tomorrow. May god give me strength", she said to herself.

She entered into the store room and turned on the lights. "Um, where did I keep the box of lights? We will decorate our house tomorrow and have fun and Matt will be home. The family will spend the last day of the year together and welcome 2012 together", Jill kept talking to herself whilst removing the pile of blankets, folded on the top of each other. "Um.." Jill said while bending down. "A rat crossed her path and Jill screamed out of fear. "What was that? Wait, a rat? In the store room. Oh god! Oh god!" Jill started screaming. "Where did it go? I need to find it and oh god, the stuff. It must have created a nest or maybe reproduced", Jill placed her hand at the back of her head in panic. "Matt, Matt come home fast", she said while placing the blankets separately and hesitantly removed the curtain that was covering the locked window but to her relief, there was no sign of rat's shelter. "Maybe it's just one" she said to herself while her eyes were searching the room from top to bottom. While the rat was away from Jill's eyes, the doorbell rang.

Jill jumped outside the store room in a hurry and went to open the door. She was so scared of the tiny creature in their home that she forgot to check who was outside but fortunately, it was Matt. She instantly hugged him and said "Thank god, you came! Thank god! Thank god!" she kept saying it breath after breath. Matt held her tightly and replied "What happened? Tell me!" to which Jill answered, "Rat..Rat in our store room", her mouth was half opened while pointing towards the room. Matt entered the lobby and went in the hall, kept his bag on the dining table and hanged his jacket on the door handle. "Tell me, where did you see it?" asked Matt while folding the sleeves of his shirt. Jill tiptoed and came towards him, "I..saw..near the stool, near the blankets..it vanished in the air". Matt looked at her with confused expressions, "Vanished? In the air? Jill?"

Jill shut the main door and explained him the incident, "I don't know where it went? I have no guts to enter inside the room knowing the rat might be there. And probably there's a hole we don't know anything about". Matt showed her the palm sign and entered inside the store room. After trying all the possible ways to catch it, he said "Babe, I think we should put live trap here. It is impossible to catch a running rat". Jill agreed with the idea, "But we don't have it". Matt looked at Jill and questioned, "But I remember we had one" to which Jill answered "We did but the door it had, broken. Later, I threw it away". Matt nodded his head, tried to understand what Jill was saying. He was too tired and his body was taking all the energy out of him in order to function. "Okay, we will get a new one and keep it here, next to the gate. It will take down the mice", Matt mocked. "Wait, we have mice in our home?" asked Jill. "You knew about it?" Jill continued speaking. "Sh..", said Matt and came near Jill to hug her. "I was just kidding", he whispered in her ears. "I'd be lying to say this isn't the best opportunity to hug you", said Matt while tightening his hands. Jill replied while hiding her smile, "You always do this to me knowing that I am too scared of rats". Matt took a deep breath and stood still holding her in his arms. "What about your dinner? You had it?" He questioned while trying to make an eye contact with her. "Yep, ordered savoury food. A good large pizza", she replied while boasting, using her shoulders. "Without me?" he asked. "You didn't have anything?" she asked. "I had..but..not pizza", he said while raising his shoulders and making dramatic face. She again hugged him and said "We can have that anytime you want. But this peace that I am breathing in right now, is eternal, my friend". Both of them enjoyed an amorous moment with each other.

"Okay, you're taking a leave tomorrow", Jill asserted. Matt kept looking at her before opening his mouth. "Ah, I don't want to hear anything except a yes!" Jill continued speaking. Matt opened his shirt's sleeves and opened his almirah to take out his night dress. "What? Ain't you going to answer?" asked Jill while blinking her eyes continuously. "You said I can't say anything else", Matt answered while looking at his thermal pyjamas. "What do you mean? No day off tomorrow?" asked Jill. Matt scratched near his hairline and replied "Of course, it's a yes!" Hearing which, Jill came running towards him and said "You're going to get a tight one from me". Both of them ended up laughing. "We will go out, have fun but with this I remember..Ayra didn't come back to invite us", said Jill. "She didn't?" asked Matt. After saying this, Jill sat on the edge of her bed and started thinking about something. "What happened?" asked Matt. "Um.. I want to talk about today" said Jill. Matt wore his pyjamas and brushed his hair saying "Yep, go ahead!" Jill took a pause before speaking again "I had a very different feeling today. Everything was just abnormal. Like I have a mixed feeling. My throat almost choked and the worst part is, the more I tried to reach out for help, the more I sank in the soil". Now, there are certain perks of dating or marrying a writer…You get the details.

Matt's face expressions changed completely. "What are you saying?" he asked with the confusion in his eyes, trying to understand the logic behind the words. He was down on his knees and kept his hands on Jill's legs. "Tell me!" he asked with all his attention on whatever Jill was about to speak. "I had weird dreams last night", Jill spoke while choosing her words carefully. "I know about it, then?" said Matt while rubbing her legs softly. "Then what happened Jill?" Matt put emphasis on his question. Jill looked in Matt's eyes and described the incidents briefly. "According to Ayra, she came to our place, rang the bell but no one attended her", said Jill while massaging her cheeks. "And?" asked Matt while moving his head slightly down. "And what happened?" he was expecting Jill to answer as quickly as possible because the silence was killing him from inside. "Tell me, Jill. You were out?" he questioned sternly. He was losing his patience while worrying about his wife. Jill cleared her throat and said "I don't remember her ringing the bell. I never heard it!" Matt's expressions changed from curiosity to worriedness, "Were you far from the main door? Is our doorbell working?" Matt questioned to hear a positive response. Jill nodded her head, afraid to speak anything she wasn't able to believe in. "I didn't hear the bell and when I called to check with Ayra, she said they stood outside our home for a while and left the place after waiting..", Jill replied while rubbing her hands because of nervousness. "Jill, look at me. Is there anything that is troubling you? Anything that you are not telling to me?" asked Matt. "Umm..you need to live a day with me to understand the scenario. I cannot explain everything using the words", replied Jill while hiding her tears. "Babe! Look at me. I am really not understanding what are you saying? Please help me with it", said Matt. "I will tell you", said Jill with a smile. "For now, let's sleep it is 1:30 already and I am too tired", Jill continued speaking.

Matt kept looking at Jill and said "I am worried for you, darling. This should be the first thing we discuss in the morning". Jill agreed while unfolding the blanket and laying it flat. "Definitely!" replied Jill with a smile. "Cuddles?" she questioned to see Matt's reaction. "I am in", replied Matt while smoothing out the wrinkles by running the hands over the surface of the sheet. Jill jumped on the bed to enter in the blanket and hugged Matt. "Turn off the lights", she added while shutting her eyes. "Tricks, huh?" Matt teased while flipping the switch. "I think I just saw a rat on your side", said Matt while pulling his socks up. Jill started jumping on the bed after listening to the statement. Matt started laughing helplessly. He kept his hand on his stomach in order to control the breathing pattern.

Jill looked at him with a surprise and dramatically jumped on him saying, "You!" Matt rolled out of laughter and fell on the bed. Jill put her hand on his chest to feel the rhythm of his heartbeat. "I am grateful to have you", Jill said. "You are one of my best decisions", said Matt while keeping his hand on hers. She slept next to him while putting one leg on his torso and other folded inside. "I love you. Good night", said Jill and closed her eyes. "Where's your eye mask?" asked Matt. "In the cupboard and I have no energy to even lift a finger. As caring Matt was, he removed the blanket and went to get the mask. He opened the cupboard, took it out and made Jill wear it. "You have to keep your surroundings dark in order to have a good sleep", said Matt while moving his fingers through her hair. He covered her with the blanket and said "I will sleep till noon, tomorrow. It's been ages we haven't spent holidays together at home", he said.

"Excuse me, we? If you'll sleep this late then how are we spending time together?" questioned Jill while removing the eye mask from one side. "Babe, you'll be seeing me in the house for a whole day. What's better than this?" asked Matt. Jill covered her eyes back and faced the side of the wall. "Ungrateful people. Good night". Matt hugged her tightly and kissed her hair saying "I love you, sweet heart. Please wake me late".

It was somewhere around 02:42 in the night, Matt seemed to be in his deepest sleep. Jill removed Matt's right hand from her shoulder and walked out of the room. She wasn't born insomniac but from past few months, her sleep cycle was disturbed. While walking on her toes, she entered into the kitchen to drink some water. "I could have drank it from my side table but no, Jill, you have to roam like this at night", she whispered to herself. "I desperately want to sleep today. I am so tired", she said and slowly went inside her room. "Avoid making any noise Jill" she murmured and opened the drawer to take out a pill.

While coming back to the kitchen, she felt a strong gush of wind near her legs. As she was moving ahead, the energy was getting stronger. "How come only my legs are feeling this?"

she said to herself in a nervous tone. She immediately went inside the kitchen, drank water from her glass and swallowed the pill with it. "I won't be able to explain this to Matt. Its better I sleep before anything else happens. Maybe there's something wrong in this house. Maybe we should talk to get our home purified", she said all the words she could think at that point of time to herself. She entered inside her room, held the blanket, left her slippers on the floor and sat on the bed. She slowly made way in the blanket using her legs, next to Matt', aware of not waking him up. After facing the wall, she kept imagining all the possibilities of what happened to her just a minute ago. "May be there's a ghost or maybe someone did black magic or maybe I walked in my sleep", she kept whispering.

It was 3:00 and her eyes caught attention of the alarm clock. The minute hand was moving really slow as if time had stopped. She folded the blanket in her hands and tightened the grip. Her eyes were continuously watching the movement of the clock and suddenly she started to feel cold. It was a teeth biting situation. She felt as if someone had kept a dry ice on her hands and the navel. Looking at Matt's eye, she touched his hand using a finger. It was unexpectedly warm, Jill's eyes opened wide. "How is this possible?" she said in an audible tone. The room had all the reasons to be warm, the sticks were burning in the furnace, the chimney was working fine, infact she was in the same shoes as Matt was, an hour ago. "What is wrong with me?" she questioned herself.

As night grew darker, the intensity of the coldness surrounded her completely. The pill she took to make her sleep was working in a reverse direction. Her eyes weren't shutting even for a moment, the fear immensely covered her mind and she was blinded by all the negative possibilities. The blanket was not protecting her anymore, it became chilly and frosty. It felt as if the energy was drained out of her body and she was finding it so hard to even call her husband's name who was sleeping next to her. The thermal which was sufficient for the weather initially, was inadequate against the biting cold surrounding her. The intense cold seeped through the jacket and her fingers, despite being covered, started to feel numb from the cold. Struggling to maintain the body heat, she tried to shield herself by covering the body with every possible thing around her including the pillow, but couldn't find any protection. The exposure of her body to extreme cold created a dangerous and uncomfortable environment.

She kept looking at Matt but as expected, he couldn't sense anything in his sleep. "M.a..t.ttt", she spoke while gathering all her strength in one place. "Ma..ttt.." she repeated but this time her voice sounded airy. "Maattttttt", she screamed at the top of her voice. Hearing this, Matt woke up immediately. He looked at her, unable to recognize where he was. "Wh..What happened Jill?" he questioned while touching her. When the warm hands touched her, the relief that she got made her shut the eyes in peace. "Jill? Jill look at me? What happened?" asked Matt while sitting on his knees, next to her. "Why are you shivering? What happened?" Matt kept on asking, trying to understand her situation.

After a few seconds, the abnormal rush in Jill's body stopped. He hands stopped shivering, the lips turned back to normal state and tears started flowing out of her eyes. "Jill", said Matt after placing his hand under the chin and said "Babe, what just happened?" After several questioned been bombarded on her, she shifted her position, used her hand's support and sat on the bed. He kept a pillow behind her back in order to provide her support and asked, "Now tell me! Why are you worried? What happened?"

Matt kept looking at her lips in a hope to hear her answer all the questions. "Please tell me!" Matt asserted while wiping her tears. Jill bit her lower lip and replied "I do not know", she paused and then continued speaking "I d.....how I started feeling cold. Extremely cold! Even after covered under a blanket, my toes and fingers were burning in ice. My hands..", she explained while looking at her hands. "My hands were shivering, no-no-no-no actually they were swinging in the air because of the biting cold", she completed her sentence. "Biting cold? But babe, our room is warm comparative to the environment outside. How can you feel this way?" he questioned while raising his eye brows. "I am telling you I was feeling cold", she became defensive while pulling the blanket close to her chin. "I am telling you it was really-really cold but suddenly, every bad feeling stopped", she made her last statement clear by elaborating it. "I mean why I would lie to you?" she almost broke in tears while explaining.

"Okay! Okay! Come here", Matt said while wrapping her in his arms. "I am sorry, I misunderstood. Forgive me". Jill kept holding the corner of her blanket, staring at the wall, resting her head on his chest. "Believe me", she said to make sure he understood the depth of her emotions and words. "I do!" he said while bending his neck to kiss at the tip of her forehead. She slowly moved her left hand around his neck and closed her eyes. It was 04:02 AM, she slept after thinking about the incident for some time. After two hours of restless sleep, she woke up. It was 06:00 AM and this time, she felt warmth around her. Matt's right hand was holding her from the waist and they had slept in the same position from the time of last discussion. She gently removed his hand and the blanket. Removing the knots from her hair, she opened the first drawer of the bedside table to take out the claw clip. After tying her hair neatly, she came out of her room, turned on the kitchen lights and gently pulled the curtains apart from the middle. Snow was visible everywhere. The houses were covered white, the roads were empty and wind seemed to blow from house to house.

She went near the kitchen slab, opened the faucet and washed her hands. After pouring the water in the mug, she started looking for the coffee jar. "I want to drink it in order to feel the positivity", she said to herself while remembering every bad incident that had happened to her over the past six days. "Last day of the year", she said while yawning and stretching the body. After walking near the calendar hanging near the main door, she crossed '31st December 2011'. "2012, it is", she said while putting the tip of marker in her mouth. While checking the calendar, she realized about the newspaper, "The delivery person hasn't dropped the newspaper at our home".

Entering the kitchen, she kept the jar on the stove, poured the water from the mug in it and left it to boil. She later used the spoon to take some coffee out of its jar and poured it on one side of the boiling water. After adding some white sugar, she took out the milk from the fridge to mix with it. She yawned again while scratching her back and looking out the window. "The weather is so beautiful but I need to see the sun again. The clothes aren't drying, the shivers run down the body any time of the day, the oak sticks are out of stock sometimes and the festive activities run late because of it", she said while looking at the boiling jar. She simmered the gas and went inside the common washroom in the hall to freshen up. After spending approximately ten minutes inside, she came out and went straight into the kitchen to check the coffee. She turned off the stove, poured the coffee in the mug and stirred it well using a spoon. Taking the mug in hand and phone in another, she sat on the corner of sofa set and placed the mug on the table.

Her mind was racing with every second, thinking about what all could have happened. "I need to buy colors for the girls. I hope they have slept peacefully", she said and walked to climb the stairs. On reaching at Macy's door, she knocked it and then entered inside. "Girls!" she said and went near the bedside. Macy looked at her with half opened eyes and replied, "Mom, we have holidays. Please let us sleep". Jill gave the girls a soft caresses on their cheeks and then walked to the window. While adjusting the curtains, her eyes caught attention of the colors spilled at the corner of the room. "These girls!" she murmured and started to arrange the colors one by one in the plastic box. "What are they trying to make? Mandala?" she asked herself while holding the A3 sized sheet. "Hmm..seems good", she said and kept the stuff on Macy's study table.

Walking down the stairs, she was looking at her cup that looked half empty. "But, how's that possible?" she said to herself while running to see the cup. "Who drank that?" she said while checking the structure of the cup. "Matt", she called his name and entered the bedroom to see if he was playing a prank on her. To her surprise, he was sleeping on the bed. "Matt, it isn't a joke", she said and went near him to take a proper look. Matt was actually sleeping and he was really finding difficulty in opening the eyes. "Matt? Did you drink my coffee from the cup?" she questioned but in a soft tone. He shook his head in order to convey his answer and pulled the blanket to cover his face. Jill kept her left hand on her mouth. She was shocked.

"Did I forget to fill the cup?" she said and went inside the kitchen to check the jar. Opposite to her expectations, the jar was empty and placed near the sink to be washed. She went near the sofa and checked the mug again. "But..How..", she said to herself and tried to categorize that incident in the normal course of events. "Maybe I don't remember clearly. Maybe the coffee was this much in the cup from the start and I must have not paid attention", she said and sat on the sofa while her left leg folded and the right one, touching the floor. She took her phone in hands and started opening the notifications by tapping on them. "I have started forgetting things and this is not a good habit. I should really work on myself", she said while taking a sip of her cup. "Ah, turned cold", she gave a remark and again took a sip.

"We will go out today. I will tell Matt to take us all out and spend time with us. I mean the day should be utilized well plus who have seen tomorrow?" she said while taking cup in the kitchen. "Everyone is going to wake up late and I feel super hungry. Let me make something for myself", she said while opening the jar of cookies. "Jill, bad idea. What if children saw you eating these?" she said and closed the lid.

"Avocado Toast", she said while making a snapping sound using index finger and thumb. She took the packet of loaf, checked the expiry date. "One day to go!" she said while opening the seal. She took out the toaster from the almirah and put the breads in it. After toasting them to a certain level of crispiness, she took them out in a plate. After cutting the avocado in half and removing the pit, she scooped the flesh in the bowl. While mashing the avocado with fork until it reached to smoothness stage, she sprinkled some salt and pepper to taste. "Ummm, I think I have a lemon in the fridge", she said and opened the fridge door. The lemon was placed on the top part of the door. She took it out, cut in halves and squeezed one half in the bowl. Taking the toasted bread slices in her hand, she spread the mashed avocado evenly over it. After topping with some cherry tomatoes and drizzling the olive oil, she placed it in the plate. She repeated the steps and placed the slices in the plate one by one. "Seems sufficient for me", she said while using the entire mixture from the bowl and keeping it near the sink. Placing the toaster back in its place, she shut the kitchen almirah and came outside with the plate in her hands. "Smells nice!" she exclaimed and kept the plate on the center table. She sat on the same side of sofa where she was sitting while drinking her coffee and took the first bite. "Mouthwatering", she said while taking the second bite. "Children will go crazy after tasting such a good dish", she said and enjoyed the taste. "Ah, I am full", she said after completing the toasts from her plate. "Time for some work now", she told herself and stepped out of sofa. After leaving the plate on the dining table, she went to the balcony at the back side of her home. She was rearranging the items in the corner while humming. There was a voice that was easily heard from a distance, as if someone was singing too close to her ears. She stopped humming in order to listen to the sound more clearly. The voice stopped. She again started humming and again heard a strange sound.

Jill held the gate of the balcony and looked around but unfortunately found nothing. As she was looking here and there, a shrieking voice of someone laughing was audible. It was not just one person, there were two different voices which almost shocked Jill. While trying to figure out the source of the sound, it stopped again and this time for a while. Out of two different sounds, one was similar to what she heard when she was in her car on that day. She immediately went towards the switch board and turned on the lights. She stood still to make sure what she experienced in the last few minutes was real or not. To cross check, she again started humming but there was no other sound audible. After waiting for few minutes, she shut the balcony door after her and entered in the hall.

"Strange!" she said and went inside the bathroom to take a shower. While standing in front of the mirror, she kept gazing at herself. "What have you become, Jill? You were never like this", she said to herself and opened the tap. The water kept flowing and she cupped her hands to fill the water in it. After splashing several times on herself, she turned the tap off and removed her clothes to take a shower. She turned it on and adjusted the water temperature. By testing the intensity with her hand, she allowed the water to thoroughly wet her body. She massaged the shampoo into her scalp using the fingertips and rinsed it thoroughly. After wrapping her hair with the towel, she wore the bathrobe and came outside the bathroom. Opened the slippers in the corner and went inside her room. She took out a blue colored turtle neck and leggings from her almirah. She unwrapped the towel and hanged it on the door knob. Running her fingers into her hair, she applied the conditioner and came outside the room. She tied her hair with a clip and came outside the room. It was 08:00 AM by the clock, she removed the curtains from the hall windows and went upstairs to wake the girls up. "Macy, Laxie", she called out their names for two times. After removing the blanket from their faces, she said "Girls! Wake up and get ready. I am preparing your breakfast and once dad is ready, we will go out to have fun", she explained. Macy jumped with an excitement in her voice "Yaee. Mom, where are we going?" she questioned. "Look at the energy of this girl", Jill replied while running her hands in Macy's hair. "Mommy, love me too", Laxie said. Jill kissed Laxie on her cheeks and said "Now, wake up. Its 08:00 already and snow has covered all the areas outside our home in a very beautiful way. "Mommy, you smell nice", Laxie commented. "I have just come out of shower and had my breakfast. So I am totally ready!" Jill replied.

Laxie and Macy sat on the bed to question "Where are we going?" Jill stood up to remove the curtains and replied "We are going to someplace new. Forget this, quickly tell me what do you want to eat in the breakfast? I had avocado toasts just now". Laxie raised her hand and said "Menu, please!" Jill smiled and sat next to her saying "Um.. Okay, so you could have Smoothie bowls, which is healthy by the way, French Toast and I am not making an avocado thing again because I just did, Regular omelette and we can totally add cheese to it, burritos which you haven't demanded from a very long time, pancakes for some sweet taste, waffles but I don't know how to make them taste up to the mark and noodles which is everyone's favorite". Laxie raised her hand and said "I am going to eat noodles and smoothie bowl" to which Macy added "Same but different. Add cheese to my omelette and please, I need orange juice too". Jill acted as if she was writing something on the hand and replied, "Noted, Ma'am. Please clean up and I will be waiting for you, downstairs". "And Mom, we have enough colors so you don't need to buy them and we are going to make some good art on the wall today", said Macy. Jill smiled and took an exit from the room.

"Matt is still sleeping. Well, he was not able to sleep well last night so it's okay. Let him take an hour more", she said while tying her hair in the form of bun and clipping the edge. "God must give me an award for working so hard and not even paying attention to anything my boss says. Such non-toxic life", she said while looking at the ceiling. She took out the juice cans and poured the orange juice in two glasses and kept them on the dining table. After taking out carrot, broccoli, pepper, cabbage, capsicum and tomatoes from the fridge, she shut its door. She took out the packet of noodles, tore it from the corner and took out two pieces and kept it on the slab. While chopping the vegetables on the board, she placed the water to boil on the stove. After boiling the noodles to get tender, she took it out in the jar after removing the water. While putting the large skillet over medium heat, she put sesame oil in it. After adding the minced garlic and ginger to mix, she put the vegetables and shook the skillet to let them mix. She added the ingredients including salt, pepper and chilies. After a few minutes of cooking, she added the boiled noodles and mixed them well. She garnished the green onions and added some vinegar in it. She took a single strand of noodle for taste and added some extra salt to balance it. "Yum!" she said to herself and served it in a dish.

After placing it on the dining table, she again went back to the kitchen to prepare the smoothie. "How will they drink smoothie and juice together? What a unique combo!" she said and took out some berries from the fridge. "Um, milk, yoghurt, a banana, pineapple and spinach", she recalled and kept putting the items on the slab. "I think we are running out of bananas. Now worries, berries and pineapple will work", she said and added the ingredients in the blender and blended on high until smooth. "Oh, I forgot to add the nuts", she said and opened the bottom right drawer below the slab. She took out some nuts and placed them inside the jar. After adding more water to match the smoothness required, she added the maple syrup in it. She poured the mixture in the glasses and kept them on the tables.

Meanwhile, she saw Macy coming downstairs. Jill looked at her and welcomed her with the open hands. "Come here, darling. Breakfast's ready for you. Eat some nuts before you start with anything else", said Jill. "Mommy, have you added cheese in my noodles", Macy asked. "No, I have added a special ingredient and you'll love it", replied Jill. "But Mommy, I told you to add it", Macy scorned. "But darling, Lax do not prefer it. Plus, I couldn't make it separately. But I can grate cheese on your share", Jill tried to convince her. "Um, let me taste it", said Macy while holding a fork. "Aha, first nuts!" Jill warned. "Where is Laxie?" Jill questioned while looking upstairs.

"She's searching for her dress to wear", Macy said. "Okay! You should have helped her", said Jill. The moment Jill completed her sentence, Laxie opened her room's door. "Come, sweetie", said Jill and placed two plates in front of the girls. She served the noodles in them and placed the smoothie glasses next to each plate. "Girls, how will you drink juice after this heavy smoothie?" Jill questioned. "Mommy, I can drink orange juice whenever I possible. I so love it!" Macy exclaimed. "Mommy, I won't be able to drink the juice. Please take it away", said Laxie. "Okay!" Jill emphasized on the word while speaking and kept the glass on the slab. "Now, taste it and tell me how it is?" questioned Jill. Laxie took the nuts and ate them, she later used the fork to move it in the noodles in clockwise direction. Macy took a sip out of her smoothie and then put the fork in her plate. "What if I add ketchup in it?" said Macy while looking at Laxie. "Why can't you eat things as they are, sometimes cheese, sometimes veggies? Ugh", questioned Laxie while rolling her eyes in clock wise direction.

"Girls! Stop throwing tantrums and start eating before it completely gets cold", said Jill. "Mommy, you won't eat?" asked Laxie after taking a sip from her smoothie. "I told you before that I have already taken Avocado toasts. I woke up really early today", said Jill. "But you should taste this, its yum", said Macy while joining the thumb and index finger into a circle. "Is it?" Jill's eyes shined. "Let me get my fork as well", said Jill and tiptoed towards the kitchen. "Wait for me", she continued speaking and came back running. She placed a small amount of noodles on her fork and twirled them around to eat "Yummy. I am a good cook", she boasted. "Don't make me eat continuously. Finish your breakfast fast. We have to go out and you have to decorate the wall as well", said Jill while pointing towards lobby near the main door.

The girls finished their breakfast and left the plates on the table. "Girls! Do not run and sit back here", said Jill. "We don't have time", said Macy and went upstairs. "Keep your plates in the sink", said Jill while sitting on the chair. Macy and Laxie went inside their rooms and came running back a minute later. "Give me those brushes", said Laxie while running. "No, I have a good design on my mind. Let me carve it", said Macy in her defense. "You want to carve? How can you do that on a wall?" asked Laxie. Jill was hearing conversation of both the girls while holding the dirty plates in her hand.

"Okay, so I will tell you the design", said Macy and stood near the wall. "Do not fight", said Jill and kept the stack near the sink while looking at the clock. "Time to wake Matt", Jill said and went inside her room. "Matty, its 10. Wake up! We have lots and lots of work to do today", said Jill while throwing her hands up in the air. "We will be having lunch outside" Jill whispered in his ears. With a groggy stretch and a yawn, he rubbed his eyes and blinked blearily, his expression was a mix of confusion and reluctant awakening. "Two minutes more" said Matt while showing a 'V-sign' to Jill. "No, No", you have slept more than me but look at my energy. If I can, you can", said Jill while sitting on his back. She touched his right cheek and said "Baby, wake up. You promised an entire day with me and now look at you. Please don't waste it in sleeping", said Jill.

After a minute or two, Matt finally opened his eyes shifting his posture and took a big yawn. "Give me some time at least", he said. Jill pressed her hands on his chest, gave him a kiss on his forehead and touched his arms. "You're my home, you know that right?" said Matt while kissing her hands. "So, if something is said in the morning, it can really make someone's day. Shall I really start believing in the quote?" asked Jill. "You haven't yet?" asked Matt. "Nope! Of course No!" Jill simpered. "Now, come on. Wake up and enter into the bathroom. Tell me what you will have in the breakfast", she continued speaking. "You, maybe!" Matt replied. "Matt, I am serious", she said. "Well, I am not sure if I want to eat anything right now. Just a glass of milk will work for me", said Matt while opening his almirah. "Okay, Sir!" she replied while throwing off dust from her clothes. "That was a task for you?" asked Matt with a surprise. "Ahem, hmm", said Jill and came out of the room.

"Girls, what have you made?" asked Jill while keeping her hands on her waist. "Ahan, this looks beautiful", she said while looking at the wall. It was a flower like pattern, a central point is small, intricate star. Surrounding this, there were concentric rings. The first ring was made up of small, repeating triangles that formed a flower like pattern. The next ring featured the interlocked hexagons which created a layered effect. The outermost ring had additional floral elements, overall symmetrical and design. "It's Mandala", Macy said while showing her fingers dipped in the colors. "This is lovely! You are such an amazing artists", said Jill while staring at the wall. "Mommy, I gave it a last touch", said Laxie. Jill nodded and looked at the wall again. "Thank you, Mommy", said Macy and continued working on the wall. "Finish this quickly. We will be going out for shopping", said Jill. "Dad is almost ready", she continued speaking and went to the kitchen, opened the fridge door. After pouring the milk in in the glass, she kept the can back to its place. She placed the mug on the slab and cleaned it with a soft dry cloth. Placing the pot on the stove, she poured the milk in it and turned on the heat. After stirring for a while with a wooden spoon, she removed the pot from the stove and transferred it to the mug. Keeping the mug on the table, she called Matt, "Babe, milk is ready". "My turn!" said Macy while shifting Laxie on the other side. "No, it's mine", said Laxie while pushing her. "Girls!" Macy yelled. "Do not fight", she continued speaking. The moment Jill warned them, they started washing their hands normally. The girls went to their rooms after washing their hands.

Jill kept the nuts in a bowl, next to the mug on the dining table and went inside the girls' room to clean it.
While picking the items scattered on the floor, she said "These girls make me run on my toes every time. Nobody can tell that the room was clean a day ago and what is this toy doing on the sash panel". She dusted the shelves, picture frames, light

fixtures and the furniture. For hard-to-reach places, she used a step stool. After sweeping the debris and filling the dustbin, she came downstairs and kept it on the corner. "Will throw it away once the bin is full", she said to herself while removing the gloves and washing her hands. Matt came out while fully placing his T-shirt's collar button. "Jill", Matt called her name. "A minute", Jill replied while showing her index finger. "No wonder why women take so much time in getting ready", Matt said to himself while throwing his hand in the air. He took out his phone from the pocket and searched for the available tickets for his flight to Chicago on 2nd January 2012.

Jill came to Matt and questioned, "What happened, Sweetie?" to which he replied "I forgot to inform you about the meeting I have on 2nd next year, well technically, yeah! So I am booking a flight for the same". Jill kept looking at him and said "Okay, and you want me to?" hearing this Matt replied while completing her sentence, "Come, yeah of course!" Jill looked at him and replied "I can't, you know that! I will be having office and from two days, I am on leave". Matt hugged her and replied, "We will have a quality time". Jill nodded and replied "Definitely! But I can't. But, oh, we can plan it the next month. I will definitely take a week off, what say?"

Matt sat on the chair and picked the nuts to eat. "I am putting on a dress and replied "Oh, what about I wear a sequin dress?" Matt looked at her and replied, "You can dress as you like. Everything will work". Hearing this, Jill went inside the room and shut the door. After a few minutes, she came outside wearing a red ribbon in the hair, light pink dress, paired with matching the sandals. "You are not feeling cold?" Matt questioned. "Nope! I feel happy in this dress", Jill replied while moving her hands from top to bottom. "Please wear an overcoat, I believe you're feeling cold", said Matt. "I will take it along but definitely opting this look", she said and went inside her room. "Which one?" asked Jill from across the hall while showing the two options.

"A Burgundy one!" said Matt after pointing towards the left side. "Great!" said Jill and kept the coat on the sofa set. "Hair up or down?" Jill questioned. "No, keep them open and even ribbon isn't necessary", said Matt. She tied a wrist watch in one hand and held the clutch in another. "Please take a picture", said Matt. "You do the honors", said Jill while giving the phone to him. Matt took the phone and started clicking pictures, "One..Two..Three..Pose!" Jill looked at the camera and kept showing her teeth. "Change!" he said. "Okay, now it's already 2. Let us move", Matt said. "I am coming in two minutes", he continued speaking and went inside the washroom.

Jill climbed upstairs and knocked at girls' door saying, "Open the gate, darling". Macy opened the door and said "Come here". Jill looked at her suspiciously and questioned "What happened? Dress isn't fit?" Macy and Laxie looked at each other and replied, "We have something for you!" Hearing this, Jill became happy and asked curiously, "Tell me! Tell me!" Seeing Jill happy, Macy showed a jar to her mother. "What is it?" she asked while checking it. "It's a memory jar. All the memories that we have created are in this. The happy memories. The sad memories", replied Laxie while taking out a slip out of it. "How much we love you?" read Jill with a smile. "This is so beautiful", she replied. "But you can't open it. Read this once you're free and your mind is calmly available", said Macy while taking the slip from her mother's hands. "So is it a surprise?" asked Jill. "Definitely!" replied Macy. Laxie closed the lid of the jar after keeping the slip back in it and placed it on the table. "It will stay here, okay?" said Macy and held her finger.

All three of them went downstairs and kept checking their dresses in the mirror. Macy kept her hair open on a purple colored dress with white sneakers and brown jacket whereas Laxie on the other hand tied two ponytails on a green colored jacket and jeans with brown shoes.

"You are Beautiful", Matt exclaimed and kissed her on her cheeks. Jill blushed and both the girls put their hands on eyes as if they were not supposed to watch *'adult things'*. Trying to avoid the situation in a healthy way, Jill nodded her head horizontally and said "Let's leave." After taking an exit from the door,
Jill locked it and kept the keys inside her clutch. All four of them sat in the car and Matt turned on the ignition. He turned on the AM/FM Radio and played the song "Vogue by Madonna". After asking for like 'n' number of times, Matt didn't reveal the destination. After twenty minutes, they reached the destination and Jill's jaw dropped. "Sky chimes?" Jill said in loud voice. Matt came outside and said "Yes! After fifteen years".

When Matt and Jill were in studying in college, they used to visit 'Sky Chimes' a lot. "After so many years, being at this place, makes me feel nostalgic", said Jill. "I know!" said Matt while holding her hands. "Let's go!" he continued speaking and all of them went inside. "Are we going to eat our favorite food from the menu?" she questioned. "Only if they still have it on their list" he replied in a mocking way. She looked at the place and it was beautifully decorated with the lights. "It has changed a lot. I am absolutely amused. Earlier there were limited number of lights", she replied. Watchman greeted them and Matt pointed towards the right cornered table with a glass on its left wall, "Is that occupied?"

Matt went to the counter to fill the details and three of them sat on the designated table. "Mom, I will eat pepperoni pizza please", Macy said. "Me too", Laxie added while looking at Macy. "Stop copying", Macy said while making a face. "Stop, girls. Do not fight", Jill showed her hands to both. Matt came back on his seat and asked "So, what would you like to have babe?" while handing over the menu card to Jill. "Bagels, always!" said Jill while looking at Matt. "My favorite!" he replied. "I really hope it tastes the same", Matt continued speaking. "Fingers crossed!" replied Jill.

While going through the card, waiter came to take an order. Matt started speaking, "I'd like one plate of mayo pasta and garlic-ginger bread, one plate of bagels, and one cheesecake. Also, two glasses of red wine, please". Jill looked up at the waiter and said "One plate noodles and one pepperoni pizza". Before Jill could complete the sentence, Matt interrupted, "Babe, we have already ordered so much. Are you sure you want to add on these?" to which Jill replied "This is for the girls!" "Girls?" Matt asked, his eyebrows raised and his ears eager for an explanation. "Give us a minute", said Matt while showing his palm to the waiter. Matt bent towards her and asked, "Are you going to explain which girls you are talking about?" Jill pointed at the two chairs on her left and right, "Our girls! Macy and Laxie. They want to eat pizza and noodles".

After hearing what Jill said, Matt kept looking at her without blinking his eyes "Jill, I don't know what you're talking about.

Macy and Laxie?" Jill looked at him with a surprise in her eyes, "Matt, Macy and Laxie?" Matt patiently tapped on the table and asked "I know who they are but right now, here on this table, it is just the two of us. Only two of us. I repeat, only two of us". It was very rare of Matt to behave like that. "Why are you acting like this?" questioned Jill with an expectation to hear a positive answer. "Matt, the girls are sitting on this table. Macy, Laxie, why are you not telling your father that you are here? He is acting completely different", said Jill while looking at her left and right. "Different and me? Jill, we both came to this place, just us", Matt said while keeping his palm under her chin. "I am telling you, why you are not believing me?" asked Jill. "Macy, Laxie", she shouted on the top of her voice. Matt stood up listening to her and said "What is wrong with you, Jill? What girls and where are they?" he said while closing his fist. "Give me a minute. Waiter, Waiter. Waiter. Come here", Jill said in an assertive tone. "You can't see the other two people sitting with us, on this table", Jill said, emphasizing the word 'people'. Waiter kept looking at her and then he shifted all his attention towards Matt, "Is she making fun of me?" he asked while pointing his index finger towards her. Jill kept looking at the waiter, "Excuse me? Am I making fun of anyone here? Can't you see my two little girls?" she questioned and all the people sitting in that restaurant who could hear them, started noticing. "Sir, I am really sorry but I don't know what she is talking about. Which girls, Madam?" waiter asked while looking at her. Matt told him to leave and nodded his head, trying to make him understand that he too was judging the scenario. "Jill, look at me. You're scaring yourself. It's probably just your mind playing tricks on you. Let's not make a big deal out of it. Let's go home and grab something to eat", Matt said while trying to control the situation. "I am not imagining things, Matt and for god sake please believe me. I am not imagining anything. This is real. Girls? Why are you not saying anything?" said Jill while looking at her left. "Macy, look at me! You wanted to eat pepperoni pizza, right? Why aren't you telling him?" Jill continued speaking. "Laxie, you tell your father about this. You only told me to eat pizza and then we negotiated on noodles. We are holding hands right now. Everything. Tell him. Tell him", Jill said while raising her voice. She shifted her chair backwards and said, "Macy, Laxie. Your dad thinks I am mad. He clearly does because you both aren't saying anything. See, everyone is looking at us. Please tell him that you both are here with us", Jill kept speaking in her defence. Hearing and seeing all of it, Matt's eyes welled up but he closed his fist to control his emotions and said "Jill, let's go home. Please". He went to her side of chair and held her waist, let's go". Jill pushed him very aggressively and replied "I know what I see". She broke down in tears and starting breathing heavily. "Jill, Jill, you'll exhaust yourself this way. Please try and understand, let's go", Matt said while pushing her in forward direction. "Jill, let's go", Matt insisted after feeling Jill's resistance. "No, you are not understanding me, Matt. Out of all the people you are thinking that I am lying to you", said Jill. "Babe, let's leave this discussion here", Matt replied while pressing her back. "Macy, Laxie, let's go home", said Jill while looking near the table. **People around them were completely confused and couldn't figure out what the couple was arguing about.** "Okay, we are taking them along. Let's go", Matt pretended while looking at the same direction Jill was pointing at. "Come on, girls", Matt said. "I was joking with you earlier", Matt continued speaking while blinking at the waiter. Waiter understood the gesture and went to the counter regarding the order cancellation.

Jill started walking while stretching her arms in the left

direction, "Come Laxie. Matt, you hold Macy's hand". Matt nodded at her and took a step forward. He was constantly thinking about her strange behaviour. It appeared as if she wasn't able to find a line between reality and fiction. While thinking all of this, they took an exit from the restaurant's door. "Matt, we are hungry. Why are we going back?" said Jill. "We will take something on our way. Pizza base was out of stock here", Matt replied with a pretentious smile. He opened the car door for Jill and she immediately opened the back door for the girls. "Get in, girls", said Jill. Matt was not ready to accept the situation and seeing Jill behave really strange, made him feel helpless. As he walked, he begin to notice the weird coincidences that mirrored the events which he had neglected. "When she was telling me that she is experiencing something different. I should have paid attention", he thought while entering inside the car. Jill shut the back door and sat on her passenger seat. "We will eat something very quickly. We are starving!" Matt heard her speaking. He drove the car for a while and stopped at the corner.

That place was known for its variety in street food. Small shops. At one side of the street, there was a cozy bakery with a striped awning displays of freshly baked bread, pastries and cookies in its window. The warm, inviting scent of vanilla and cinnamon wafted put on the street. Next to it was a quaint café with a few tables placed under a canopy. Little snacks, coffee and tea were visible on the three tables. "Matt, we can go there", said Jill while showing her index finger in the shop's direction. Without saying any word, Matt stopped his car in front of the shop and said "I am bringing everything you want to eat". He tried to maintain his usual attitude in front of the world. He went to the shop's counter and said while looking at his car, "Two pizzas, One cheese pasta", that's it. The shop manager noted his order and told him to wait for ten minutes to which Matt fake smiled. He again looked at his car and was not even feeling shocked to see Jill talking in the air. Her mouth was moving continuously and with every second, Matt was getting flashbacks.

Matt and Jill were in a healthy relationship and later got married after maintaining an understanding. Even after two years of their marriage, Jill was not able to conceive. She intensely wanted to be a mother and always imagined a beautiful family since their dating days. The couple went through countless doctor visits, fertility treatments, and emotional ups and downs. Their home had seen moments of hope, from long nights of shared tears to hopeful discussions about the future possibilities. After their last round of treatment, they decided to take a brief break from the rigorous schedule of appointments and procedures. They focused on simply being together and finding joy in their daily lives by spending weekends in hiking, cooking meals together, and rediscovering the small pleasures that brought them closer.

One fine day, Jill's prayers finally got answered. She took another pregnancy test and it came positive. The couple was happy. After nine beautiful months, Jill became a mother of twin girls. Tears of happiness streamed down Jill's face as the news sank in. "Girls are healthy", doctor said. Both of them named them 'Macy and Laxie'. They transformed their home into a space for the new addition. The girls were proved lucky for them. Even Jill's parents who were unhappy because of her marriage, came to visit her at their home. Life was perfect. Few years went happy, all of them lived their best times. On May 5th, the family planned to go on a picnic, after all it was girls' birthday. Matt booked skiing tickets and the family decided to take a road trip on a sunny afternoon, driving along a scenic highway. Macy was not up for skiing so she asked Mary who was Jill's elder cousin to join them. Macy and Mary used to play doll house together. On her special request, Matt and Jill picked Mary on their way. All five of them headed toward the destination. The car was filled with the hum of a playlist, Macy, Mary and Laxie were sitting on the backseat of the car. Macy was holding a picnic basket with her favourite cucumber sandwiches, fruits and chocolate cake. After driving to a distance, rain started to pour down heavily and visibility gradually decreased. Matt was driving very carefully, but the roads became slippery. Jill was trying to digest the sudden change in the weather because when they left their home, sun was shining as bright as possible but later, the storm was visibly approaching them. Suddenly, another vehicle skidded on the wet road and collided with their car. The impact was jarring, and the car spun before coming to a stop. The family was shaken but, fortunately their seat belts and airbags protected the couple from severe injury. Matt and Jill quickly checked on the twins and Mary but they were gravely injured. Emergency services arrived promptly and everyone was taken to the hospital for precautionary checks. Jill was holding the girls throughout, she even forgot her own bruises. After a thorough examination, it was confirmed that three of them were not breathing. They were heavily wounded and because their heads touched the roof of the car and to the window, Macy suffered from a brain haemorrhage, Laxie was declared brought dead and Mary's spine broke gravely. Jill held their hands till Matt forcefully pulled her apart. The accident was a frightening experience for the family and for the next few days, Jill remained lost. She almost forgot to speak and was never ready for any kind of conversation. Silence covered their home and turned it into a 'house made of bricks and rocks'. After rigorous therapy sessions and talks, Jill finally showed the signs of recovery. Grieving time was over and she finally started accepting her fate. The couple even talked about it for hours and after many crying episodes, Jill decided to move on. They stopped talking about the incident and whenever the topic even came in their conversation, Jill seemed mature enough to pass through the reality check. Both of them continued living their lives in a moderately healthy way. Matt had no idea even in his dreams that she was living a life in her parallel universe. She never mentioned anything about the girls in front of him and now, everything was off track, yet again.

"Sir, your order", the boy said while placing the tray in front of Matt. He paid the bill, took the tray and went inside the car. Jill immediately took pizza slices and placed on the backseat and Matt kept watching her. She then took the pasta box and pressed her fork against the corner of it. "You aren't eating anything?" asked Jill while looking at him. "I am not hungry", said Matt while trying to hide his tears. "Are you sure? We booked a table because we were hungry. You remember?" Jill tried to explain the validity in her point. Matt nodded his head and said, "Yes. But I don't feel like eating now". Jill looked at him and then at the backseat while smiling. Matt was anxious seeing Jill behave like that. "Give me the paper plates now", said Jill while looking at the backseat. She kept the slices on the tray and told Matt to return the tray back to the shop owner. According to Jill, the girls had eaten the pizzas but in reality the slices were not even touched. "Feeling full?" asked Jill while looking at the backseat.

Matt kept his hand over his mouth and opened the car gate.

He was constantly failing to recognize this new version of his wife. He went straight to the owner and placed the tray on the table and returned back. He turned on the car and kept his eyes glued on the road. Jill was laughing and talking but Matt was not involved in any of it. He was trying to absorb what was happening around him. He applied brakes as they reached their home and Jill kept talking in the air. She went inside their home and Matt stayed on his seat. He leaned his head on the steering. Thoughts kept racing inside his head and his eyes started to become red. "I can't stay like this, I have to get her out of the whole situation", he said to himself and opened the car door. He went inside the home and found Jill sitting on the couch.

"What took you so long?" she asked while checking her phone. "See, Jacob hasn't answered my leave request. Am I fired?" she questioned dramatically. Matt held Jill's hand and started speaking, "Whatever I am going to tell you now, you need to understand and accept. Okay?" Jill nodded her head with suspicion in her expressions. "Everything that happened in the restaurant was not right. We both went on a lunch date to have a quality time but it turned out really different", he said and continued speaking, "And we…", he took a pause, "have lost our daughters in a car accident three years ago. Are you getting me? There is no Macy or Laxie in this house". Hearing this, Jill took a step back, indicating her refusal to engage in the conversation. "Listen to me. You are imagining things, which are not real. You have healed from the loss", Matt started giving her positive affirmations because he was in no position to push her back into that same labyrinth in which she was stuck, three years ago. "We live in this home, just the two of us. Only us", he put emphasis on every word while speaking. Unable to set herself free from his hands and the words, Jill started pushing him away. She started screaming and pushing her elbows against his chest. "Do not lie. Macy, Laxie, come downstairs", she yelled while looking upstairs. Matt counter attacked on her using his words in order to make her realise that she was hallucinating because of the loss. After several failed attempts of convincing her, she felt a wave of dizziness and fainted in his arms while holding her head from one hand. Matt tapped on her cheeks, calling out her name. She was unresponsive but breathing. "Jill, Jill, Jill. What happened to you?" Matt said while making her lean on the sofa. He gently tilted her head to ensure her airway was clear. On sprinkling cold water on her face, she stirred and regained consciousness, blinking her eyes open. "Jill", he kept repeating her name until she was in the position to understand what was happening with her. **She took a few sips and started to feel a bit better, though she remained shaky. As she sat on her sofa, she started to remember what they were talking before she passed out. Her head started to pain very badly. "Jill, are you okay?" Matt questioned very politely. "Where is Macy and Laxie?" she stood from her place while asking. "Macy, Laxie, Mommy is coming", she said in a loud and clear voice. She immediately rushed upstairs, followed by Matt, "Jill, stop". Jill opened the door of Macy's room and the view was shocking.**

Dust had settled thickly over every surface, and the air was filled with a musty, stagnant color. The room was enveloped in shadows and silence. Jill took a step inside the room and found a rat crossing her path. She screamed on the top of her voice. The intensity was so sharp, Matt had to cover his ears. The lock was rusted and its hinges were corroded, placed on the top of the table at the right side. The moment she took the second step, a rush of stale air escaped from the room, mingling with the scent of old paper and mildew. The room was cloaked in a thick layer of dust, cobweb covered windows and curtains were hanging on the brink. The air was heavy.

The couple closed the rooms after the girls passed away and since then, Jill never moved a single thing from any place to another. "Ma..cy", Jill whispered. Matt was standing still behind her with the teary eyes. She turned around and pushed Matt to take an exit from the room. After opening the Laxie's door, she saw the same view.

In the center of the room, an old armchair, faced a large, ornate fireplace. The fireplace was filled with ashes and cobwebs, and the once-grand mantel was then covered in a thick layer of dust, with a few scattered, brittle letters and forgotten trinkets resting atop it. "They gave me a jar today. Where is that jar? Jar?" said Jill while making an exit from Laxie's room. She searched the entire room of Macy but could not find it. The overall atmosphere was one of melancholy and mystery. She fell on her knees, grieving. Her hands turned grey and clothes became dirty because of the dust.

"Matt, I can show you their sippers. We bought them together", she said while running downstairs and then towards the kitchen. She opened all the drawers but there was no sign of them. Matt kept looking at her with heavy eyes. "I am not lying, they even painted the wall today. It is so beautiful, let me show you. She went to the lobby and pointed towards the wall. The moment, her eyes fell on the wall, she realized the wall was a simple, unadorned expanse of pale, neutral color. Its surface was smooth and even, with no visible texture or pattern. "Painting?" she questioned herself and then made an eye contact with Matt. "I am not lying. They even demanded new colors to paint. Where did the painting go?" she said to herself. "We can find the colors in their rooms", Jill said and climbed the stairs to enter into Macy's room. Matt followed her and said, "Jill?" to which Jill replied "Matt, I am not lying..I need to find the colors..Then you will know". She opened the table's drawer and there were some old brushes. The color palette was empty and dry. Colors were not there. "I can show you their school bags, I even pick them up from the school. Their uniforms. Id cards", saying this, Jill rushed towards the store room. According to her, the girls used to hang their cards at the backside of the door, on the hook. "There it is", she said while seeing the cards. "See, I told you that I am not lying", she said while taking out them from the hook. She showed the card to Matt, "See. See". She took a look at the card and was taken aback, "Batch 2007-2008", she spoke in a loud voice. Her eyes turned red, hands started shivering and she moved her hand inside her hair. "I am not lying, Matt", she kept repeating. Matt was looking at everything she was doing. "I can show you the photo that I clicked when we went for skiing", Jill said while opening her phone's gallery. She kept scrolling and there was a picture but Macy and Jill weren't there. The picture had snow but there weren't any girls. Jill kept refreshing the page but the picture was still the same. "Matt, I might have not included them in a frame. You know, I am such a bad photographer", Jill said while leaving the phone on her table. "We..We.. went to a restaurant and we had frankies. I can show you", said Jill while taking out the bill from her purse. She immediately dialed the restaurant's number and enquired "H..Hi, This is Jill. Ma'am, I came to your restaurant this week..I want to get the cameras checked.." After several tries, the person on the other side of the phone agreed. Jill smiled and kept the phone on speaker, "Ma'am, please confirm who all visited the restaurant" to which the woman on the speaker replied "Ma'am, I can't share the confidential details but I am certain there were no children in our restaurant at that time you mentioned". Jill disconnected the call and threw it on the sofa. "Let it out", Matt said in a very audible tone. Jill slowly started to accept the reality. She kept crying, tears were flowing from her eyes continuously. Matt came near her and wrapped her around. Both of them stayed on the floor for hours. "They are dead", she finally said the words. "Matt, they are no longer alive with us", she said to him. "Photo? I found a photo when I was cleaning the floor", Jill said while opening the side drawer of the TV cabinet. "This photo", Jill said while handing a burnt piece to Matt. "Jill, you burnt this photo after the accident. You told me this was the way to move forward. You even hid all the photo frames which had our daughters, in the almirah", Matt explained and brought a glass of water and made her drink from it. "Babe, take a sip", he said. Jill held the glass and started drinking. Matt was finally understanding everything so he got up, took out his phone and called Jimmy. The phone kept ringing but there was no answer. After trying her second number, a boy answered. "Hello?" Matt said. "Hello?" a reply came. "Can I talk to Jimmy?" Matt questioned. "One second", the boy replied and after a few seconds, Jimmy answered. "Jimmy, Matt this side", Matt said. There was a pause for a moment. "Hello?" Jimmy replied. "I wanted to confirm the reason behind your absence", Matt mentioned. With all the hesitation, Jimmy replied "I am scared to enter your house. Ma'am is possessed", Jimmy said and disconnected the call. Matt redialed the number, but it was turned off by then. He then called the therapist she was taken to in the early stage of experiencing the loss.

The doctor answered the call, "Hello? Hi Mrs. Martha", Matt greeted while going towards the main door. "Hi, Mr. Charles.", Martha replied. There was a loud music in the background,

"Are you out somewhere?" Matt questioned while pressing his index finger in the other ear. Doctor took a pause and after few seconds, she replied "Yes. Eve Party" to which Matt questioned "Can I have a moment with you?" saying this, Matt explained the entire episode to her.

Hearing his ordeal, she started explaining "Umm..I remember texting her this week for I guess, two times but didn't get any response. With what you are telling, sounds like she is having 'Schizophrenia with Acute Migraine' which is a chronic and severe mental health disorder that affects how a person thinks, feels and behaves. Earlier when I met Jill, she was dealing with the denial. With the repetitive sessions, her denial turned into anger which was more or less a blame game on the accident and later her mind shifted to the depression phase. We stopped her medication when we finally saw some signs of recovery in her. Like you are saying, if now she has finally understood that the girls are gone that means she is on the first chapter of accepting the bad phase. In her case, she is experiencing hallucinations, auditory and visual, alongside several headaches. Even if she come back to normalcy for a short period of time, she faints at the end to suppress the pain or run from what her surroundings is trying to tell her. She knows the reality in the back of her head but denies it on the front foot and is actually making stories of her own". Matt was listening to the doctor conscientiously. "Did she mention about the severe headaches?" to which Matt replied, "Yeah, but not in an elaborated way. She mentioned about the headache". "Nausea or vomits?" asked the doctor. "Um, no. I don't think..She might explain you better", he replied with patience in his voice. "Okay. I am.. Umm..I am not in the city right now. Is it possible for you to bring Jill at my hospital day after tomorrow?" doctor said. "Yes. Absolutely", Matt replied.

"Okay. See you!" said the doctor. "Thank you!" Matt replied and disconnected the call.

Matt went straight to Jill and hugged her. He was experiencing mixed emotions in the moment, knowing that she was dealing with all of it, alone. "We will fix everything", Matt whispered in her ears while holding her closer to himself. "I love you!" he added. "Sleep now", he pressed her hands softly and took her to the bedroom.

On 2nd January 2012, Jill was taken to the doctor and her diagnosis was done. Doctor wrote the medicine and gave it to Matt. She explained the entire condition to the couple and Jill agreed for the therapy. After a few months of visits, Mrs. Charles began speaking normally.

The couple enjoyed multiple holiday trips together, which allowed them to spend quality time and strengthen their bond. During that period, Jill decided to dedicate more attention to her writing career, which likely involved setting new goals and pursuing her passion more seriously. At the same time, Matt remained occupied with his responsibilities in marketing, where his dedication and effort were recognized. His commitment paid off with a significant achievement, a double promotion, reflecting his exceptional performance and the value he brought to his role. As a result of the positive changes and accomplishments, their lives gradually settled back into a routine that felt normal and balanced, after all the previous disruptions or challenges they faced.

On one fine day, the couple was present in the balcony, seated side by side on a weathered wicker bench, basking in the warm glow of the late afternoon sun. Jill's face was tilted upwards & her eyes were closed. "Let me bring some snacks from the kitchen", Matt said after keeping the magazine on his side table. He wore his slippers and went inside the kitchen.

Jill stayed in the same position for few seconds and then opened her eyes, looked at her right side and spoke softly, "Girls, come here".

****

Special Thanks to Anumita (Illustrator) & Dev Verma (Photographer) for contributing in this book.